SOCCER
MADE SIMPLE

FOR PARENTS & SPECTATORS

A QUICK GUIDE FOR UNDERSTANDING
TERMINOLOGY AND RULES

Dennis H. Reid

Habilitative Management Consultants, Inc.

Published by

Habilitative Management Consultants, Inc.

PO Box 2295

Morganton, North Carolina 28680

Copyright © 1996 by

Dennis H. Reid

ISBN 0-9645562-1-9

Library of Congress Catalog Card Number: 96-77166

Printed in the United States of America

Produced by

PPC BOOKS

Westport CT 06880

DEDICATION

This book is dedicated to all the parents, family members, and spectators who support America's youth in the game of soccer.

PREFACE

Soccer Made Simple was written for people interested in watching, understanding, and enjoying youth soccer. The book is not intended, however, for individuals who have in-depth experience and familiarity with the game. Rather, the information in the following pages is designed for persons who have little or no experience in having played soccer while growing up, yet have become interested in the sport as adults. Those of us who fall in the latter group of interested soccer fans represent the vast majority of adult soccer spectators in the United States.

For the most part, increased adult interest in the game of soccer has developed for one reason—our children and other family members have begun playing the game. In fact, soccer represents the fastest growing participant sport among America's youth. As children and adolescents have begun playing soccer at record levels, more adults have started attending and watching soccer matches. Unfortunately though, because of a lack of history with the game, parents and other spectators often experience difficulty understanding the sport in which their children and friends are participating. Difficulty in understanding what is taking place during a soccer match can seriously impede a spectator's enjoyment of the match, as well as a parent's ability to support a son or daughter's involvement in the game. *Soccer Made Simple* was written to provide parents and spectators a quick means of understanding the game of soccer as played by children and adolescents throughout the United States.

In a manner designed to be readily understood by even the most inexperienced soccer spectator, *Soccer Made Simple* describes typical positions and responsibilities of players on a soccer team as well as common rules and penalties that are integral to most soccer matches. Perhaps most importantly for spectator understanding of ongoing soccer play, soccer terms and phrases frequently heard during youth matches are also explained from a lay point of view. My hope is that by reading information in the following pages, parents and spectators will noticeably increase their enjoyment with the game of youth soccer.

Dennis H. Reid

ACKNOWLEDGMENTS

I have learned about the game of soccer from far too many people to recognize each person individually. However, there have been several people who have been especially instrumental in teaching me about the game. In particular, I express sincere appreciation to the players on the Burke Blast Soccer Teams coached by Lonnie Suiter and Keith Ross, respectively. Similarly, the players on the Freedom High School Soccer Teams coached by Rob Wilcher and David Fletcher have played vital roles in teaching me what the game is all about.

I also express appreciation to Helen Reid and Marsha Parsons for providing valuable assistance in the preparation of this book.

TABLE OF CONTENTS

Chapter 1

SOCCER MADE SIMPLE
FOR PARENTS AND SPECTATORS

INTRODUCTION

Soccer is the fastest growing participant sport among
America's youth. Record numbers of boys and girls are
currently playing on soccer teams throughout the United
States. In response to such pervasive interest, new soccer
programs are being established almost continuously, ranging
from city recreational teams for 4- and 5-year-olds to entire
interscholastic conferences for high schools.

Due in large part to the growth in the number of children
and adolescents who play soccer, there has been an increase in
the number of American adults who *watch* soccer. One
segment of the adult population in particular for whom soccer
has become a major spectator sport is the parents of the kids
who are playing the game. Essentially, the growth in number
of youth playing soccer has been paralleled by the growth in
parents watching soccer.

The vast majority of parents who watch their sons and
daughters play soccer have never played soccer themselves.
Their interest in watching soccer often has little if anything to
do with a love for the game per se, or even interest in the game
itself. Rather, most parents watch soccer matches for one
reason: to observe their son or daughter participate in the
activity. The parents are interested in supporting their children
in various endeavors, and soccer is an endeavor in which their

1

children participate.

Parental interest in supporting their children's participation in different activities by attending the activities is a natural interest, and one that is usually beneficial for the overall development of children. In the case of soccer however, a somewhat unusual situation develops. Specifically, because most parents of soccer players in the United States have never played soccer themselves and have no background in the game, the parents are trying to support their children in an activity about which the parents have little knowledge.

The lack of soccer knowledge among parents of soccer players is not a major hindrance to the development of soccer skills among the parents' sons and daughters. Coaches are available to teach soccer skills to interested players. Although historically there has been a serious lack of knowledgeable soccer coaches in the United States relative to the number of youth interested in soccer, the number of skilled coaches is growing. However, the lack of soccer knowledge among parents of soccer players can be a serious detriment to the parents. Lack of knowledge about what is taking place during a soccer match—or perhaps what the coach wants to be taking place—can seriously detract from the enjoyment a parent obtains from watching a match. Lack of information about what occurs during a match also impedes a parent's ability to interact meaningfully with a son or daughter about what happened during a match. In short, it is difficult for a parent to fully support a son's or daughter's soccer participation if the parent has little understanding about the sport in which the youth participates.

Most parents and other interested spectators can gain a basic understanding of the game of soccer simply by watching a lot of soccer matches. The primary objective in a soccer match is quite straightforward: get the ball in the opposing team's goal more times than the opposing team gets the ball in one's own goal. Typically though, scoring goals involves less than one percent of all the activity occurring during a soccer match. To really enjoy a soccer match, as well as to understand and enjoy a son's or daughter's participation in the match, a parent needs to know what is taking place during the remaining 99% of the match. To know what is happening on the soccer field, a parent needs to understand team strategies and tactics as well as one-on-one matchups between individual players (and especially one-on-one competition involving a respective son or daughter).

> *Scoring goals constitutes only a small fraction of the action during a soccer match. To really understand and appreciate soccer, spectators need to understand what is occurring during the other 99% of the match when goals are not being scored.*

One of the best ways for parents and spectators to acquire soccer knowledge is to attend soccer matches and listen to what coaches say to players, and to what players say to each other. However, learning about soccer by listening to interactions among players and coaches requires a familiarity with soccer terminology, and most adults in the United States do not understand soccer terminology. Soccer, like any sport, has its own unique terms and phrases—terminology that leaves many new soccer spectators wondering what is meant by various instructions, commendations or criticisms they hear from coaches and players. Hence, it would be quite helpful if spectators could quickly learn the most common examples of soccer terminology. Having a good grasp of basic soccer terminology enhances spectator understanding and enjoyment of soccer matches. More importantly from the perspective of parents, familiarity with soccer terminology allows parents to better understand what their sons or daughters are doing, what their coaches want them to do, and how well they are doing it.

Purpose of

Soccer Made Simple for Parents and Spectators

The purpose of **Soccer Made Simple** is to provide parents and other soccer spectators a basic understanding of the most commonly used soccer terms and phrases in the United States. The terminology to be described is based on 15 years of experience on the part of the author as a soccer coach, referee, parent and spectator. Additionally, lists of terms have been generated by recording the most frequently used soccer expressions during hundreds of soccer matches involving youth from preschool ages through high school.

The primary intent of **Soccer Made Simple** is to enable soccer spectators to better understand and enjoy the game of soccer, as well as to enable parents to more effectively support their son's or daughter's participation in organized soccer. It should also be noted though, the intent is not to provide detailed instruction in all aspects of the game of soccer. Such a purpose is well beyond the scope of this book, and probably beyond the scope of any text. Like most team sports, a seriously in-depth knowledge of soccer for those adults who have never played the game can only be obtained through intense study that involves for example, watching matches and practice at all skill levels, reading about the game, and discussing the game with knowledgeable soccer enthusiasts. Nevertheless, interested soccer parents and spectators can significantly enhance their knowledge about the game, as well as their ability to support youth participation in the sport, by acquiring an understanding of the popular soccer terminology described in the following pages.

Understanding soccer terminology increases spectator understanding and enjoyment of the game, and enhances parental support of youth participation in soccer.

Organization of Text

This book is organized in three sections. Section 1 describes the basic positions of the 11 players who constitute a soccer team during a match (Chapter 2). Section 1 also describes popular terminology used to describe soccer playing fields (Chapter 3). A detailed description of soccer field parameters (length, width, playing surface, etc.) is not provided though, because such information is not needed by most spectators to understand and enjoy the game. However, because much confusion often exists among spectators regarding references to aspects of the field, such as the *goal area* versus the *penalty box*, a few simple descriptions are provided. Additionally, some common misconceptions and inaccurate references to the field are described in more accurate soccer terms. Section 1 likewise provides a description of the more common soccer rules and penalties (Chapter 4) that frequently cause confusion, and at times disgruntlement, among American soccer spectators.

The information provided in Section 1, as well as to a large extent in the remaining book sections, pertains to *outdoor* soccer. Rules and penalties pertaining to *indoor* soccer are not covered. There is however, considerable overlap in the rules as well as common terms and phrases between outdoor and indoor soccer. Nevertheless, because the game of soccer is played much more frequently outdoor than indoor, and because rules for indoor soccer can vary significantly across different indoor soccer associations, leagues and tournaments, indoor soccer will not be addressed in this text.

Section 2 of *Soccer Made Simple* describes in nontechnical language the most common terms and phrases heard during soccer matches. For organizational purposes, the terminology described in Section 2 is separated into three chapters (Chapters 5 - 7). Chapter 5 describes terms used with offensive plays—plays designed to set up and actually score goals. Chapter 6 focuses on terms used to describe defensive plays, or those plays designed to prevent the opposing team from setting up and scoring goals. However, it should be emphasized the distinction between defensive and offensive plays is a fine one; good defensive plays help establish a soccer team's offense and good offensive plays help protect the team's defense. The third chapter in Section 2 (Chapter 7) describes miscellaneous jargon that is unique to soccer and frequently heard during soccer matches, such as popular commendations used by coaches and players for praiseworthy soccer play.

The final section of *Soccer Made Simple*, Section 3, provides a listing of selected readings for those readers interested in obtaining additional information about the game of soccer. Respective readings provide a more in-depth discussion of soccer rules as well as more general information about game strategy and suggestions for improving specific soccer skills of young players. Section 3 also presents an alphabetized index of the terms described in Chapters 2 - 7. The intent of the index is to provide soccer spectators with a quick reference for finding an explanation of terms as they are encountered, such as while watching an actual soccer match.

A Quick Start on Using This Book
To Understand Soccer As a Spectator

For those readers interested in quickly obtaining information about soccer terminology for use in watching soccer matches or talking to soccer players, a *quick start* for using this book can be obtained by skipping certain chapters and going directly to chapter sections that describe popular terms. Specifically, the reader in a hurry can go immediately to the sections in Chapters 5, 6, and 7 that describe the most commonly heard terms during a soccer match. Gaining a quick understanding of the terms and phrases in Chapters 5 - 7 can significantly enhance one's understanding of what is taking place during a soccer match. Readers also may find it useful initially to take this book with them to soccer matches and use the index to quickly look up specific terms as they are heard during a match. However, to gain a more complete understanding of what takes place during a soccer match from a spectator standpoint, it is recommended that readers who use the "Quick Start" method later go back through the other book chapters on soccer positions, the playing field, and rules and penalties.

Section 1

Common Soccer Terms Relating To

Player Positions, The Playing Field, and Rules and Penalties

Chapter 2

COMMON SOCCER POSITIONS: NAMES AND RESPONSIBILITIES

When a soccer spectator is interested in a particular player during a soccer match—such as a son or daughter—it is most helpful if the spectator knows what position the player is playing. It is likewise helpful if the spectator knows the general responsibilities of the respective position.

This chapter describes the 11 basic positions constituting a soccer team. The intent is to provide the reader with an awareness of the most common types of soccer positions, what the positions are typically called, and the primary responsibilities of the positions. Understanding the basic types of positions as described on the following pages will generally allow the reader to observe any organized soccer match in the United States and have a good idea of what position a particular player is playing and what constitutes her duties.

Before describing the 11 basic soccer positions, it should be noted that in some youth soccer associations there are less than the traditional 11 players on the field at any one time. In many recreation programs for younger players, the number of players is reduced in order to enhance player participation in the action of the game as well as to allow more instructional activity by coaches. For example, it is common to see only nine players on each team on the field during a match for players less than nine years of age. However, because the standard number of players on a team is 11, which represents the number of players on almost all teams above the elementary school-age level, the following discussion will pertain only to teams involving 11 players on the field.

Basic Types of Soccer Positions

When attempting to understand basic soccer positions, a forewarning is in order. Although this chapter will allow spectators to understand the basic soccer positions and accompanying responsibilities, spectators should not expect to totally understand the position of each soccer player during every soccer match. Difficulty in understanding all soccer positions is to be expected for two primary reasons. First, different coaches use varying types of line-ups and strategies across and within matches. Each line-up and strategy can affect the types of positions filled by various players as well as the players' responsibilities. Second, the terms used to label or describe each position on a soccer field can vary widely; one position may be called three or four different names. To help understand such variations in player positions, this chapter first presents the most common types and names of soccer positions, followed by a description of variations on the most common positions and respective names.

There are four basic types of soccer positions: (1) goalkeeper, (2) defensive players, (3) midfielders and (4) forwards or offensive players. Figure 1 illustrates a basic, and relatively common, configuration of these four types of positions on a soccer field.

Goalkeeper

The easiest type of position for most spectators to recognize and generally understand is the *goalkeeper* (also frequently called *keeper, keep, goalkeep* or *goalie*). The goalkeeper's main responsibility is to do just what his name implies: protect or *keep* the goal by keeping the soccer ball out of the goal.

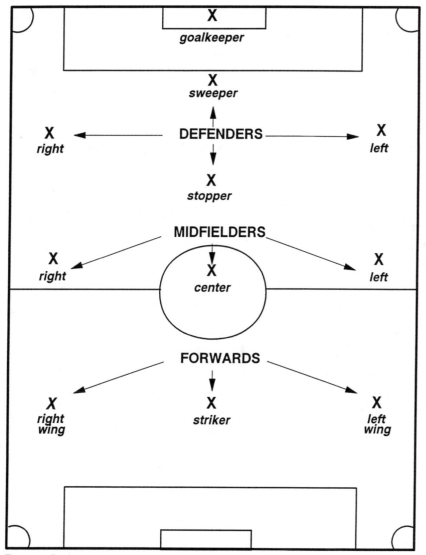

Figure 1. Basic positions on a soccer team (the positions represent the team defending the goal at the top of the page).

The keeper is the only player who may use her hands to play the ball on the soccer playing field. The keeper can use her hands to catch or pick the ball up from the ground for example, when the ball is in her team's *penalty area* (see Chapter 3 for elaboration of the penalty area, also called the *penalty box*). There is one rule though that prohibits the keeper from using her hands to play the ball even when the ball is in the penalty area: when one of the keeper's teammates deliberately kicks the ball to the keeper. In such a play, the keeper can only play the ball with her feet. The latter rule causes some confusion in soccer matches because it is a relatively new rule. Previously, the keeper could play the ball with her hands if a teammate deliberately kicked the ball to the keeper. Currently, if a goalkeeper does use her hands to play the ball in the penalty area when a teammate deliberately kicks her the ball, a rule infraction occurs and the opposing team is awarded an indirect, free kick (see Chapter 4) from the spot at which the keeper first touched the ball with her hands.

SPECIAL SPECTATOR NOTE
The rule regarding a goalkeeper not using her hands when the ball is sent to her by a teammate does not apply to throw-ins (Chapter 4). When a teammate is throwing the ball back onto the field after the ball has gone outside the field of play, the teammate can throw it to her keeper and the keeper can play the ball with her hands. Likewise, if a teammate sends the ball to the keeper with her head or off of her chest, the keeper can play the ball with her hands.

Defensive Positions

Immediately in front of the goalkeeper are the *defensive* players, or *back line*. The defensive players' main responsibility is to defend the goal by preventing the opposing team from shooting the ball at the goal. In the team configuration noted in Figure 1, the defensive players include the *sweeper, stopper,* and *left* and *right* defenders (**note**: to distinguish left side versus right side positions, picture standing in front of the goal a team is defending—the goal at the top of the page on Figure 1—and facing the field; left side positions are on the left and right side positions are on the right).

As just noted, soccer positions are referred to by different names by various coaches, players, spectators, etc. Such variability is particularly the case with defensive players. For example, the *left defender* may be referred to as the *left fullback,* or simply *fullback* as well as *left outside back* or *left back.* Presented below are the most common names of each of the basic defensive positions on a soccer team, as well as a very brief summary of the primary responsibilities of each position.

Defensive Soccer Positions	
Position	**Primary Responsibility**
Left defender (left back, left full back, left outside back)	Guard opposing right forward; prevent shots from left side of goal
Right defender (right back, right fullback, right outside back)	Guard opposing left forward; prevent shots from right side of goal
Sweeper (sweeper back)	Guard any opposing player who breaks open behind all other defenders—similar to a single free safety in American football; take control of the ball when it goes behind all other defensive players
Stopper (stopper back, center fullback, center back)	Guard opposing center striker; prevent shots from in front of the middle of the goal

As noted in Chapter 1, designating soccer positions as strictly defensive and offensive can be misleading. Soccer is a fluid game and essentially any position can assume an offensive or defensive role depending on a particular play or game strategy. To illustrate, on a number of teams, defenders are expected to *make runs* (Chapter 5) up the field to maneuver into a position to receive the ball for a shot on goal or to set up a teammate for a shot on goal by passing the ball to the teammate. In these situations, defensive players assume an offensive role. Likewise, at times forwards are expected to guard an opposing player who makes a run even if the forward must go with the opposing player the length of the field and as such, become a primary defensive player. Hence, the responsibilities noted in this chapter for various soccer positions should be considered as common, primary responsibilities and not as sole or exclusive responsibilities.

Midfield Positions

Immediately in front of the defensive players (Figure 1) are the *midfielders*, or alternatively, *halfbacks*. Figure 1 shows three midfielders: a *left midfielder*, *center midfielder* and *right midfielder* (or alternatively, *left halfback*, *center halfback* and *right halfback*). Many teams also employ a four-midfield set-up, involving two outside midfielders (left and right) and two center midfielders. When four midfielders are used, typically teams eliminate the stopper position from defense or a forward position from offense (see next paragraph). Midfielders have a dual responsibility: supporting the defensive players *and* the offensive players. An easy way to conceptualize midfielder roles is they are responsible for playing the ball in the middle part of the field. In this capacity, midfielders are expected to play both an offensive and a defensive role. Offensively, midfielders are usually concerned about getting the ball to the forwards in a position for the forwards to get a good shot on goal. Midfielders are also expected to fill an offensive role by getting open for shots on goal themselves. From a defensive perspective, midfielders are expected to move back toward their own goal and support the defenders when the defenders need help in preventing the opposing team from getting in a position to shoot on goal.

Offensive Positions

The final type of soccer position is filled by the offensive players, or *front line* (again, see Figure 1). The two outside offensive players are called the *left* and *right forwards* or alternatively, *left* and *right wings* or *wingers*. The offensive player in the center is called a *striker* or *center forward*. Some teams employ four forwards, involving two wings and two center strikers (usually by eliminating a midfielder or stopper position) whereas other teams use only two forwards, either involving two wings or two strikers. Additionally, at times teams will change their offensive line-ups in terms of the number of offensive players during the course of an ongoing soccer match.

As referred to earlier, the primary job of the offensive players is to maneuver to get shots at the goal, and get the ball in the goal net (i.e., score). In the most simplified version, wings are expected to advance the ball up the wide or outside parts of the soccer field and then pass the ball to the striker(s) in the center part of the field in front of the goal for a good shot on goal. However, with good soccer play, the responsibilities of the forwards are much more varied, with players changing roles and positions on the field as opportunities arise in an attempt to out maneuver the defense.

Chapter 3

THE SOCCER FIELD:
BASIC FACTS AND COMMON MISNOMERS

From a spectator perspective, one generally does not need to know much detail about a respective field on which a soccer match is played. What one does need to know about the field per se is usually apparent after watching a few matches on different fields. Variations in field conditions and how the variations may affect the game are rather straightforward. Extremely wet fields with puddles of water can slow a game and make play sloppy. Poorly groomed fields with tall clumps of grass or weeds can make controlling the ball difficult and result in player miskicks, bad passes, etc. In contrast, artificial surfaces and well groomed fields with short grass can speed movement of the soccer ball and the game itself.

In addition to variations in playing field conditions, the size of a field can affect play in a manner that is usually rather apparent. The size of the field can be an important issue because soccer fields across the United States vary greatly in their dimensions. Actually, many youth soccer matches in America are played on fields that were not originally designed for soccer. Many matches are played on fields designed for American football and are significantly shorter and narrower than fields designed for soccer.

When fields on which soccer matches are played are smaller than true soccer fields, such as converted football fields, soccer matches can be affected considerably. For example, small fields often have the effect of causing crowding of players on the field such that there is reduced space for skillfully passing the ball from teammate to teammate. Crowding can also have the effect of making the match more physical simply because players are more likely to physically contact each other due to reduced space in which to maneuver.

Beyond the playing conditions and size of a given soccer field and how these factors can affect play, there are some basic technical aspects about fields that, when understood, can enhance spectator understanding of the game. There are also some common misnomers when referring to aspects of a soccer field. This chapter briefly describes the more relevant technical aspects and common misnomers regarding soccer fields in the United States.

Key Parts of Soccer Playing Fields

Before describing the main parts of soccer fields from a spectator standpoint, one very common misnomer warrants clarification. Soccer fields are typically not called *fields* in many places outside the United States. To be technically correct, fields are referred to as *pitches.* However, a "soccer pitch" is a term quite unfamiliar to most spectators in the United States, and is a term rarely used even by soccer players in this country. For this reason, it is suggested soccer parents and related spectators not worry about referring to a soccer field as a pitch. In all likelihood, as soccer becomes more "Americanized", the term "pitch" will disappear from use essentially altogether, replaced with the more common reference to a soccer "field". Throughout this book soccer playing areas are referred to as soccer fields.

An illustration of the basic parts of a soccer field is presented in Figure 2. The diagram presents parts of the field using the technically correct terms. However, many of the parts of a soccer field as presented in Figure 2 are mistakenly

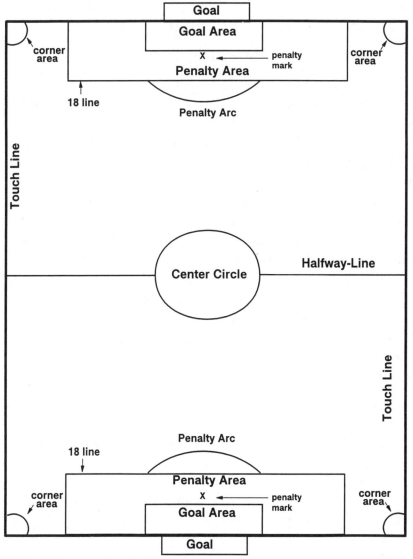

Figure 2. Key parts of a soccer field.

referred to by other names by spectators in the United States. Important points regarding key technical parts of a soccer field are summarized in the following paragraphs, followed in turn by a review of common misnomers about soccer fields.

The Penalty Box

As illustrated in Figure 2, the penalty area (also referred to as the *penalty box* or simply the *box*) is the area just in front of each goal. From a spectator standpoint, there are three key points to be aware of regarding the penalty area. First, and most readily apparent, is the effect of fouls or penalties committed by players inside the penalty box area (hence, the name *penalty* area). All major fouls or rule violations occurring inside the penalty box by the team defending the goal which is behind the box result in a penalty kick (also referred to as a *PK*). Chapter 4 summarizes fouls, penalties, and penalty kicks.

The second key point about the penalty area was noted in Chapter 2. To reiterate, the penalty area represents the only part of the soccer field in which the goalkeeper can use her hands to play the ball. If the keeper plays the ball using the hands outside of the box, the keeper is committing a rule violation, resulting in a free kick (Chapter 4) for the other team.

SPECIAL SPECTATOR NOTE
A point to keep in mind regarding the keeper and penalty box is that it does not matter whether the keeper is in or out of the box, but whether the ball is in or out of the box. Hence, the keeper may be lying on the ground outside of the box after sliding to stop the ball and she can still legally reach and grab the ball with her hands if the ball itself is inside the box.

The third key point regarding the penalty area pertains more to understanding soccer jargon heard during a match rather than to the technical aspects of the field per se. At least once during most matches reference will be made to the "18". The 18 refers to the line denoting the width or top of the penalty box—which is 18 yards from the front of the goal. References to activity at the 18 pertain to doing something in the area of the soccer field around the top of the penalty box. Some common references to the 18 along with a brief explanation as to the meaning of the references are provided below.

Common References Involving The "18"	
Reference	**Explanation**
Line up on the 18	Players should stand on the 18 line, usually before a match, so referees can check equipment, review rules, etc.
A shot from the 18	A shot is taken from the top of the penalty box
Move the wall outside the 18	A line of players attempting to block an opposing team's free kick (Chapter 4) is instructed to line up outside the penalty box

At the top of the penalty area is the *penalty arc* (Figure 1). The primary significance of the arc from a spectator standpoint is that the arc indicates where players may stand during penalty kicks. All players except the player taking the penalty kick and the opposing goal keeper must be outside the penalty area and be at least 10 yards away from the *penalty mark* or *penalty spot* (the place from where the ball is kicked). The arc marks the area immediately behind the penalty mark that is 10 yards away from the mark.

The Goal

Soccer goals are readily recognized on soccer fields and really need no explanation from a spectator standpoint. Goals are mentioned here however, because of a situation that arises when soccer matches are played on fields designed for American football as noted earlier. Soccer goals on football fields often are located below the cross bar on the football goal posts. Sometimes shots on goal will result in the soccer ball hitting the football cross bar and then rebounding back into the soccer field of play. When such action occurs with the ball, the ball is immediately considered out of the field of play (i.e., out of bounds in more common terminology) as soon as it hits the football cross bar. Hence, when the ball bounces back into the field, it cannot be played and must be started with a goal kick or corner kick, depending on which team last touched the ball (see Chapter 4 for elaboration). In contrast, if the ball bounces off the *soccer goal* cross bar or one of the two upright poles connecting to the cross bar, the ball is considered to still be on the field of play, and field play continues without any interruption.

The Goal Area

The goal area is represented by the area inside the penalty box immediately in front of the goal. This particular area does not arouse much concern for spectators during most soccer matches. The primary thing to know about the goal area is that it marks the area within which *goal kicks* are taken by the team defending the goal which is behind the goal area. Goal kicks are awarded to a team when the opposing team sends the ball beyond the *goal line* or *end line* on either side of the goal, causing the ball to be out of the field of play. The team defending the goal puts the ball back in play by placing the ball anywhere in the goal area and kicking the ball out of the penalty box. Once the goal kick is taken, no other player can touch the ball until it leaves the penalty box.

On a somewhat more technical level, the goal area also represents a part of the field in which goal keepers are afforded more protection from opposing players' physical play. For example, a referee can stop play if an opponent has sufficient body contact with the keeper in the goal area when the keeper does not have control of the ball. In such a case a free kick (Chapter 4) is awarded to the keeper's team.

Halfway-Line

The halfway-line extends the width of the field and divides the field into two halves (Figure 2). From a spectator standpoint, the halfway-line is of little consequence except for one thing: the line plays an important role in the notorious *off sides* rule. Off sides is difficult to comprehend for many spectators for a variety of reasons, not the least of which is inconsistent interpretation and enforcement of the rule by many soccer referees. Chapter 4 summarizes the key points of the off sides rule. The point of concern here is to alert the reader that the halfway-line must be considered when determining if an off sides infraction occurs.

Technical Area

Spectators are not likely to hear the term *technical area* very often in youth soccer matches in the United States. However, the term is introduced here because spectators are likely to observe the effects of coaches not adhering to rules regarding the technical area, and it is helpful to know why a respective coach has received the wrath of a referee for violating the rules. The technical area refers to the area in which the coach and other designated team officials and team players who are not participating in an ongoing match are allowed to be during the match. Various soccer associations and referees define the technical area differently such that the allowable area for coaches and related team officials differs across various matches. In general the technical area is considered to be the area designated by the bench seating along the touch line for the players (assuming there is bench seating for players, which is often not the case for American soccer fields, and particularly on fields used by younger players). The technical area also extends one yard from the end of the seating area, and up to within one yard of the actual playing field.

The overall intent of the technical area is to prohibit coaches and related team members from interfering with the flow of the match by, for example, running all the way up and down the touch line yelling to players. In this manner, the boundaries of the technical area essentially form a *restraining line* (actually, the term *restraining line* seems to be the more common term in American soccer relative to the term *technical area*). Some coaches of course ignore the rule, and particularly when they are upset about some aspect of the match. Consequently, in a number of soccer matches it is relatively common for spectators to observe a referee suspend play temporarily to caution a coach to remain within the technical area during a match.

There is one aspect related to the technical area that pertains specifically to spectators. As many spectators are readily aware, most youth soccer fields in the United States do not provide seating for spectators (or at least those soccer fields for players below the high school level). In matches played on fields without spectator seating there is a natural tendency for spectators, and particularly parents, to stand right next to the field of play in order to be close to the action of the match. Such a process causes havoc for a *linesman*, who is in essence a referee working along the touch line (see Chapter 4). The linesman has to be able to see the entire length of the field to perform her job appropriately, such as to see when the ball leaves the field of play beyond the touch line. When spectators stand next to the touch line, it is impossible for the linesman to see the entire touch line. A number of readers have probably experienced the situation in which spectators have been (repeatedly) requested by a linesman to step back away from the touch line during youth matches. To avoid upsetting referees and potentially interfering with the flow of the match, it is best if spectators adhere to the technical area rule and always remain at least one yard back from the touch line while observing matches.

SPECIAL SPECTATOR NOTE
To avoid unnecessarily upsetting referees, as well as to avoid potentially interfering with the flow of a soccer match, spectators should stay back from the field of play, and definitely not closer than one yard to the touch lines.

Common Misnomers About Soccer Fields

New soccer parents and spectators, as well as some parents and spectators who have already observed a number of soccer matches, mistakenly refer to various parts of soccer fields as they cheer for their player's team, or cheer against the opposing team. Such mistakes do not seem very important in the overall scheme of things but are nevertheless noted in this section for two primary reasons. First, when spectators yell from the stands (or frequently in the United States, from their lawn chairs or simply standing next to the field—because there are no stands for many soccer fields) and mistakenly refer to parts of the field, soccer enthusiasts such as coaches may tend to discredit or otherwise become somewhat upset with the fans. Second, players may dismiss parents' remarks that inaccurately refer to parts of a soccer field because such remarks indicate to the players that their parents do not know what they are talking about. It can also be difficult for a parent to discuss a son or daughter's play after a match when the parent mistakenly refers to parts of the field. The latter occurrence can indicate to a serious soccer player that a mom or dad does not know much about the game of soccer, and has not invested the time and effort to learn about the game. In turn, a parent's ability to maintain rapport with a player regarding soccer participation, and to effectively support such participation, can be diminished.

Confusion over parts of a soccer field occurs for several reasons. The most obvious reason of course is the lack of soccer knowledge among parents and spectators who are new to soccer. In defense of new spectators however, lack of knowledge is often exacerbated because of carry over of sports knowledge from other American sports. Most notably, many adults use jargon stemming from American football (not to be confused with the original game of football, and current international game—which is actually soccer). The latter source of confusion is compounded by the fact noted earlier that many soccer matches in this country are played on fields originally designed for, and typically still used for, American football. As also referred to earlier, it is actually rather rare to watch school teams, be they middle school, junior high or high school teams, play on anything but a football field.

To avoid field terminology mistakes for reasons just noted, the following examples represent some of the most common spectator misnomers, and the corresponding terminology that is technically correct. Whether spectators choose to use the correct terms—or soccer jargon—versus terms with which they are more familiar is of course up to each individual spectator. Nevertheless, so that an informed decision can be made regarding which terms to use, the following examples are offered for consideration.

Misnomer #1: Referring To A Soccer Pitch As A Field

As indicated previously, the technically correct name for a soccer playing area is a "pitch". As also noted earlier though, "pitch" is rarely used in the United States and is unlikely to be used much in the foreseeable future. It is recommended that readers do not to worry about this misnomer and continue thinking of a soccer playing area as a soccer field.

Misnomer #2: Referring To The Side Boundaries As Sidelines

The technically correct term for the side boundaries (the long, frequently white, lines connecting the two goal lines and forming the playing area) are *touch lines*. In one sense, the side boundaries are referred to as *touch lines* because when the ball crosses one of these lines, field players are allowed to *touch* the ball with their hands in order to perform a *throw-in* (see next Chapter) to put the ball back in play. Reference to touch lines as sidelines represents an example of confusion noted earlier with American football fields, which have sidelines for side boundaries in contrast to touch lines. Most experienced soccer players and coaches refer to touch lines.

Misnomer #3: Referring To The Halfway-Line As the Midfield Line

Referring to a midfield line represents another source of confusion about field terminology stemming from familiarity with American football. The term *halfway-line* is preferred in soccer circles. However, some justification for the term midfield line exists because the halfway-line does divide the field into two halves, and as such, extends across the *middle* part of the field. Referring to the halfway-line though as the 50 yard line—again representing confusion stemming from American football—has essentially no justification. There are no lines designated by yards per se on a soccer field except for the 18 line discussed earlier. Also, because true soccer fields are usually longer than 100 yards, a 50-yard line (if such existed

Chapter 4

COMMON SOCCER RULES AND PENALTIES CAUSING FREQUENT SPECTATOR CONFUSION

This chapter describes several common soccer rules and penalties that frequently affect a spectator's understanding of what is taking place on the soccer field. The intent however is not to carefully review all the rules and penalties of the game of soccer; such a task would make for unwieldy reading for even the most serious soccer spectator. Rather, the purpose is to describe those rules and penalties that tend to cause the most frequent confusion among spectators. Readers interested in acquiring a more detailed understanding of soccer rules and penalties are referred to the **Selected Readings** section at the end of this book.

Having a basic understanding of the rules and penalties discussed in this chapter will allow parents and other spectators to better follow the flow of a soccer match, and to understand why play is stopped, or *whistled,* by the referee at various points in a match. Understanding the common rules and penalties to be described in subsequent paragraphs also will allow spectators to know why a respective coach or player becomes upset with a particular referee's call in terms of having some idea of why disagreement exists with the call. Likewise, understanding common rules and penalties will enable spectators to determine if there is valid reason to disagree with a referee's call.

As in any sport, there is likely to be periodic disgruntlement among players, coaches, and spectators regarding certain calls made by officials during a soccer match. With the game of soccer, such disagreement is likely to be more frequent and more intense than with most other sports played in the United States. The reason for an increased likelihood of dissatisfaction with soccer officiating is three-fold. First, most spectators do not understand soccer rules, or the *Laws of The Game* as they are called in soccer. Hence, there is more likely to be disagreement between spectators and referees regarding the latter's calls because of spectator unfamiliarity with soccer rules relative to sports with which spectators have a good understanding of the basis for the referee's calls.

A rather common example of the type of situation just noted occurs with the *dangerous play* rule, which will be described later in this chapter. With the dangerous play rule, at times a player who appears to be in danger of being hurt has a dangerous play penalty called against her (i.e., in contrast to the penalty being called on the player who is likely to cause harm to the former player). Such a call frequently infuriates spectators, because it seems somewhat illogical that a player who is in a situation in which she is likely to be hurt by another player's actions should have the rule violation called against her. This situation is most frequently contested by spectators unfamiliar with the dangerous play rule when the player against whom the infraction is called is actually injured during the play. However, in such situations the referee often has made the appropriate call based on the rules because the player committed the rule infraction by *putting herself* in a dangerous situation.

A second reason for likely disagreement between spectators and officiating decisions is that currently many soccer coaches—and particularly at the younger player levels—do not have a sound knowledge of soccer rules. In the latter situation, coaches often become upset with referees when the coaches disagree with certain referee calls even though the referee made the appropriate call. Due to the coaches' lack of understanding of certain rules, they sometimes think the referees made a bad call even when the call is in accordance with standard soccer rules. When coaches become noticeably upset with a referee's call, even when the call is appropriate, spectators supporting the coach's team also tend to get upset with the referee.

A third reason dissatisfaction with soccer officiating frequently occurs is due to the relative newness of soccer in America. Because soccer is so new to many adults in the United States, a number of referees are not very well versed in soccer rules. Such referees tend to make more mistakes than referees in other sports who have a much better familiarity with the rules of the game for which they are officiating.

For each of the reasons just presented, disgruntlement with referee calls is rather common during soccer matches in this country. Having a basic understanding of soccer rules and related penalties for rule infractions as discussed in the remainder of this chapter can help reduce such disgruntlement among spectators, and increase their enjoyment in watching soccer matches. For organizational purposes, soccer rules causing frequent confusion among spectators will first be presented. Subsequently, some of the more frequently occurring penalties that lead to spectator misunderstanding will be discussed.

To reduce disgruntlement with referee calls during a soccer match, spectators should acquire a basic understanding of the most common types of rule infractions and resulting penalties.

Soccer Rules
Causing Frequent Confusion

Duration of The Match

In one sense, the duration of a match is rather straightforward: a specified amount of time is allotted to a match and the referee ensures the teams play for that amount of time. However, there are several factors associated with the duration of soccer matches that result in relatively frequent confusion among spectators regarding how long a respective match will be played. This section describes those factors affecting the duration of a match such that spectators can determine before a match begins how long the match will continue.

In order to understand factors affecting the duration of respective soccer matches, it is helpful to be aware of the basic rules about match duration. In the most common scenario, a soccer match consists of two halves of play, with equal amounts of playing time allotted to each half. In contrast to other common team sports in the United States, duration of play continues without any time outs allowed that interrupt play and cause the length of the match to continue beyond its specified duration. At times though, the duration of a match can be extended by the referee adding time to the match. The process of *adding* time is described in Chapter 7.

The most common factor associated with match duration causing confusion among spectators is that the length of soccer matches varies across a number of circumstances. Most frequently, match duration varies according to the age of the players. The general rule is that the younger the players, the shorter the duration of the match. To illustrate, a common duration of a soccer match for nine-year-olds is 40 minutes (i.e., two 20-minute halves) whereas a typical duration for high school aged players is 80 minutes. Above the high school age level, almost all soccer matches are 90 minutes in duration.

Another factor affecting match duration is the use of breaks in match play that often occur with very young players. In order to allow more instruction by coaches, as well as to enhance substitutions to allow all players on a team the opportunity to participate in a match, many soccer organizations allow a match to be broken into quarters for young and/or very inexperienced teams. It is common to see for example, a city-recreation league for players under nine years of age use a match duration of four, 8-minute quarters.

When considering how the duration of soccer matches can fluctuate as just described, it is not surprising to see frequent confusion among spectators concerning how long a given match will continue. To eliminate such confusion, typically the best thing to do is for a spectator to ask prior to a game what the rules are concerning match duration. In most cases the coach will know the duration, and in all cases the referee is responsible for knowing the specified duration of the match.

SPECIAL SPECTATOR NOTE
In order to be sure of the duration of a soccer match, a spectator should ask a soccer official prior to the beginning of play how much time will be allotted to the upcoming match.

Off Side

Probably no other rule in soccer causes as much confusion and disgruntlement as the *off-side* rule. Implementation of the off-side rule is often hotly contested for a variety of reasons. For one thing, implementation of the rule can have a profound effect on the flow and outcome of a soccer match. Most experienced spectators have undoubtedly witnessed goals discounted because a player was whistled for being off side immediately prior to the goal being scored. Discounting a goal almost inevitably results in serious discontent among spectators, as well as players and coaches. Another reason implementation of the off-side rule frequently results in confusion is the rule itself is difficult to implement accurately. Relatedly, there is often inconsistency in the way referees enforce the rule in matches played in the United States.

Before discussing the off-side rule, a point of terminology is warranted. Typically during soccer matches in the United States the off-side rule is referred to as the off-sides rule, or simply off sides. Our discussion will involve the more commonly used off-sides terminology instead of the more traditional off-side version.

The essence of the off sides rule is as follows. When the ball is kicked, headed or otherwise sent to an offensive player by a teammate, the offensive player must be in an on sides position when the ball is sent by the teammate. To be on sides, the player must have at least two players from the opposing team between him and the opponent's goal. In almost all cases, one of those players will be the opposing team's goal keeper. Hence, there must be one other player, and it is usually a defensive player such as a fullback, between the goal and the offensive player who receives the ball to be on sides. Actually in this regard, the player can be even with the opposing defensive player's position on the field and still be on sides (note: the latter *even rule* represents a relatively recent change—just to add to the difficulty for spectators in understanding the rule—relative to the more traditional rule of the opposing defensive player being behind the offensive player). If there are not two defensive players even with the offensive player or between the player and the goal, then the player should be called off sides when the ball is sent to him.

There are several key factors that affect the off sides rule. Such factors are typically best understood in terms of situations when the off sides rule as just summarized does *not* apply. Presented below is a summary of the factors that prohibit a player from being off sides even if the basic conditions just summarized exist.

Factors Prohibiting A Player From Committing An Off Sides Violation
(when a player is in an apparent off-sides position)

1. During a throw-in, corner kick or goal kick

2. If a player is in no way involved in the ongoing play even if he is in an off sides position

3. A player is behind the halfway-line (behind meaning the player is on the side of the field closest to the goal that his team is defending)

4. A player is in an on sides position when the ball is sent (i.e., kicked or headed) to him, even if he is in an off sides position when he actually receives the ball

---

Of the factors affecting the off sides rule as just summarized, #1 is the least complicated; one simply cannot be off sides on a throw-in, corner kick, or goal kick. Factor #2 is much more complicated as it requires considerable judgment on the referee's part. In brief, a referee has to determine if an offensive player who is in an off sides position yet is not involved in a respective offensive play actually: (1) gained an offensive advantage by his position or, (2) was in a position to interfere with an opponent's play. If either of the latter two situations occurred, the player would be considered off sides. Fortunately from a spectator standpoint, situations related to Factor #2 do not arise very frequently so further discussion is not really warranted at this point.

Factor #3 regarding off sides is a rather straightforward rule. However, confusion arises in some cases due to one primary reason: inexperienced referees sometimes apparently forget about the rule and do not check to see if a player is behind the halfway-line before whistling the player off sides. Relatedly, sometimes referees are not in the appropriate position on the field to adequately observe whether a player is behind the halfway-line. In either instance, mistakenly calling a player off sides when the player is truly behind the halfway-line results in a situation that usually disgruntles experienced players (and coaches) considerably.

The factor typically causing the most confusion with the off sides rule and subsequent disgruntlement among players, coaches, and spectators, is factor #4. This factor means that the determination as to whether a respective player is off sides should be made based on when the ball is kicked or sent to the designated offensive player, and *not when the player actually receives the ball.* This rule is erroneously enforced rather frequently, basically for the same reasons just noted with inaccurate referee calls when a player is behind the halfway-line—referees fail to see where a player is when the ball is kicked. Additionally, this factor is often affected by how many referees are working a particular soccer match. Typically the preferred situation is when there are three referees, one working the field itself and one on each touch line (i.e., the *linesmen*). When there are three referees, it is a primary responsibility of the linesmen to stay continuously aware, and in a position to easily see, whether an offensive player is in an off sides position during a given play. In contrast, with only two referees, both of whom work the field itself and there are no linesman per se, it is often more difficult for the referees to be in a position to adequately see if a player was off sides when the ball was kicked. In the latter case, many inexperienced referees only notice the player when he receives the ball, and subsequently make an erroneous off sides call because the referees did not notice the player's position when the ball was kicked to him.

SPECIAL SPECTATOR NOTE

One advantageous thing for a spectator to do in order to prevent some discontent when a goal appears to be scored and then is disqualified due to an off sides call is to quickly look at the closest linesman or referee immediately after the score and see if she is holding her arm up (or holding the flag up in the case of a linesman). If the referee has her arm held straight up, excitement generated by the score should be abated because an off sides call is most likely.

Throw-In

Throw-ins frequently result in referee whistles of a rule infraction, and particularly in matches involving young or inexperienced players. Actually though, except in matches involving rather skilled players, throw-ins typically have little effect on the overall flow of a match (as noted previously, a throw-in refers to when a player *throws* a ball back into the field of play after the ball has been sent off the field outside one of the touch lines). Consequently, throw-in situations should not generate very much spectator concern when an erroneous referee call occurs. However, because there are often many throw-ins during a match, and frequent referee whistles concerning throw-ins in a number of matches that result in disgruntlement among spectators, a quick overview is presented here regarding the basic requirements of a throw-in.

There are five basic requirements of a legal throw-in. Failure of a player to fulfill any one of the requirements can result in a referee whistle, with subsequent awarding of a throw-in to the opposing team. The five requirements are provided below.

Basic Requirements Of A Legal Throw-In

1. The player must face the field and the player's hands must remain on opposite sides of the ball until the ball leaves the player's hands

2. The player must remain off the field of play until the ball leaves the player's hands

3. The throwing motion must begin with the ball behind the player's head and the ball must be thrown over the head

4. The throw-in must occur from the spot at which the ball left the playing field

5. The player's feet must stay on the ground until the ball leaves the player's hands

---

The basic requirements for a legal throw-in are generally straightforward from a spectator standpoint, with two key exceptions that result in frequent confusion. The first exception is that players and spectators sometimes forget about requirement #3. The most common violation of this requirement occurs when a player is attempting to throw the ball to a teammate who is very close to the player throwing the ball such that only a short or easy throw is desired. In such cases the player taking the throw-in, or *thrower* as referred to in some situations, tends to just drop or throw the ball to the ground without starting the throwing motion from behind the head.

The second exception regarding legal throw-ins that causes

frequent spectator confusion pertains to requirement #4. Referees can be very inconsistent in how vigorously they enforce this requirement of throwing the ball in at the point at which the ball left the playing field. In the referees' defense though, their job in this regard can be rather difficult with some players who attempt to gain an advantage by moving up the touch line toward their opponent's goal before taking the throw-in.

It was noted earlier that throw-ins do not typically have a highly significant impact on a team's overall play except with more advanced soccer teams. With more advanced teams, as well as teams with older youth such as high school-aged players, throw-ins can be a potent offensive weapon. In particular, with the latter teams some players can throw the ball from the touch line to the mouth of the goal. Such a throw functions essentially like a corner kick and represents a good scoring opportunity because the ball ends up right in front of the opposition's goal. It should be noted that a goal cannot be scored directly from a throw-in however; the ball must touch another player before it goes into the net to be considered a goal. As with indirect kicks (see discussion later in this chapter) it does not matter what team the player is on regarding who touches the ball as long as at least one player touches the ball before the ball enters the goal.

One final note regarding throw-ins. A player taking a throw-in does not have to wait for a referee's signal or whistle before throwing the ball in; the player can throw the ball back onto the field of play as quickly as she can. Teams can gain an advantage by quickly throwing the ball in to a teammate and thereby catching the defense unprepared.

Free Kicks

Free kicks are awarded to a team when the opposing team commits certain types of fouls. Free kick situations occur when the referee stops play and the team awarded the free kick reinitiates play by kicking the ball from a still position. The kick is taken from the spot on the playing field where the foul occurred. In this manner, free kicks represent a type of *restart* of the game (see discussion later in this chapter for additional information on restarts).

Player fouls result in two types of free kicks with which spectators should be familiar in order to help understand the flow of a soccer match: *direct kicks* and *indirect kicks*. Major fouls, such as deliberately holding or tripping a player who has a clear break away (Chapter 5), and illegally playing the ball with the hand (see later in this Chapter), result in direct kicks. Minor fouls, such as obstruction (again, see later in this Chapter), result in indirect kicks.

From a spectator standpoint, concern really does not need to be directed to memorizing which respective types of fouls result in direct versus indirect kicks (for those readers who are interested in additional information on specific types of fouls, the **Selected Readings** section can be used for relevant discussions). It is the referee's responsibility to make the decision whether a foul represents a major or minor violation, often involving a considerable amount of individual judgment on the part of the referee. However, as exemplified in the following paragraphs, it is helpful from a spectator standpoint to know when a referee stops play and awards a free kick whether the kick will be direct or indirect. The type of kick awarded affects the game strategy of the kicking team and defending team, as well as how easy it is to score a goal with the free kick play.

Direct kicks. The most important thing to know about direct free kicks is that the team kicking the ball can score a goal directly from the kick (hence, the name *direct* kick). The most important type of direct kick, at least in terms of having the greatest likelihood of immediately scoring a goal is a *penalty* kick. A penalty kick is awarded to a team when the opposing team commits a major foul in its own penalty box. During a penalty kick, play is stopped and the ball is placed at the *penalty spot* or *penalty mark*, which is 12 yards from the goal and directly in front of the middle of the goal. One player, usually designated by her coach, takes the kick in a one-on-one confrontation with the keeper while all other players remain outside of the penalty box and the penalty arc (Chapter 3).

Although penalty kicks are typically the most important types of direct kicks, they are usually not nearly as common during a match as direct kicks taken from the main part of the playing field, which includes anywhere outside the opposing team's penalty box. Again, the main thing to know about a direct kick taken from the playing field is a player can legally kick the ball directly into the goal.

Indirect kicks. With indirect kicks, the ball cannot be kicked directly into the goal. Rather, a goal can only be scored *indirectly* by the ball touching another player before the ball can legally be sent into the goal. A player taking the indirect kick often will kick the ball lightly a few feet to a teammate who then attempts to kick the ball into the goal. In this manner the ball touches another player (i.e., the player receiving the short pass and attempting to shoot) before the ball goes into the net, assuming of course the kick is successful. Alternatively, the player taking the indirect kick may kick the ball high toward the goal with the intent that a teammate will kick or head the ball into the goal once she receives the indirect kick. From a rules standpoint it does not matter who touches the ball after the indirect kick, provided some player touches it before it goes into the goal; a player on the opposing team may be the one who touches the ball. In some cases, the indirect kick may even bounce off the opposing keeper into the goal as a legitimate goal off of an indirect kick.

To understand ongoing play on a soccer field, it can be

helpful if spectators—as well as players and coaches—know immediately when a foul is called and play is stopped whether the resulting free kick will be direct or indirect. In some cases defensive players let a kicked ball go into the goal uncontested because the players thought the free kick was indirect (and therefore the players thought the goal would not count because the ball was not touched), only to find out the free kick was actually direct and the goal did indeed count.

The expected way to know if a free kick is direct or indirect is to watch the referee's arm signal. If the referee holds his arm straight up, the kick is indirect. Further, the referee is expected to hold his arm up until someone touches the ball after the player takes the indirect kick, or the ball goes off the field of play. In this manner, players, coaches and spectators know a goal cannot be scored until the referee brings his arm down. In contrast, for a direct kick the referee is expected to point his arm directly toward the goal into which the team awarded the direct kick is attempting to get the ball. Notice, however, this means of knowing whether a free kick is direct or indirect is presented as the "expected" means of knowing. The qualification of "expected" is presented because it is relatively common for many soccer referees in the United States not to be very clear with their signals regarding direct and indirect free kicks. Players often have to ask a referee if a free kick is direct or indirect, and in such cases spectators must watch what subsequently happens to determine what type of kick was awarded.

Referee Signals To Indicate Direct Versus Indirect Kicks
Direct kick: *referee points arm toward the goal which the team awarded the kick is attacking*
Indirect kick: *referee holds arm straight up*

In addition to these primary differences between direct and indirect kicks as just summarized, it can be helpful if spectators are aware of three other rules related to both types of free kicks. First, before the ball can be kicked, it must be still (sometimes referred to as a dead ball); the ball cannot be kicked if it is rolling. Sometimes players attempt to get a free kick off quickly, before the defense has a chance to get in position to stop a shot on goal, and kick the ball before it stops rolling. In such cases a referee will disallow the kick and require that the kick be retaken. Second, the ball must be kicked from the spot at which the foul occurred. Players sometimes attempt to gain an advantage from a scoring standpoint by kicking the ball from a spot closer to the opponent's goal than where the foul occurred. Alternatively, players simply do not pay much attention to exactly where the foul occurred and kick the ball from a different spot. Regardless of the reason, the referee will typically stop play and require the ball to be placed at the appropriate location before the kick occurs. This latter rule is mentioned because stoppage of play due to violation of the rule occurs relatively frequently in many matches.

The third rule warranting attention in regard to free kicks pertains to players on the opposing team from the player taking the kick. Specifically, the opposing players cannot be closer than 10 yards to the spot of the ball until it is kicked. This rule is mentioned because players often form a *wall* (Chapter 6) between the ball and the goal and frequently set the wall closer to the ball than 10 yards. This rule is important to be aware of because referees in the United States are beginning to enforce the rule more stringently, and violation of the rule can result in a card for the offending players. As indicated in the following section, *cards* can have a dramatic effect on a match and on a soccer player.

Cards

Certain rule violations by players (and coaches) result in a referee issuing a *card* to the offending player. There are two types of cards in soccer: *yellow cards* and *red cards*. Specific rules dictate which rule violations result in yellow versus red cards being issued, as does referee judgment in conjunction with the rules. It is really not necessary from a spectator standpoint to be extremely familiar with the respective types of rule violations resulting in yellow versus red cards being issued (readers who are interested in gaining a more detailed familiarity in this respect should see the **Selected Readings** section of this book). However, it is helpful to be familiar with the outcomes for offending players and teams resulting from yellow- and red-card rules violations.

The most serious rules violations, such as deliberately hitting or spitting on a player, result in a player receiving a red card. Once a player receives a red card, she is expelled from the remainder of the soccer match. What makes a red card violation even more serious in this regard is that once the player receives the card, her team cannot replace her on the field for the remainder of the match. Consequently, her team has to continue playing the match minus a player. On occasion, several players from one team receive red cards such that their team loses a player on the field for each player who receives a red card. Hence, if three players receive red cards, then a team can only play 8 players for the remainder of the match (i.e., the normal 11 players minus 3 players, 1 for each of the 3 players who received a red card). Typically a team must continue playing minus the players expelled due to red cards as long as the team has at least 7 players on the field. If a sufficient number of players receive red cards such that there are less than 7 players on the field, the team that is short the players usually must forfeit the match.

46

Another serious consequence of a player receiving a red card is that not only is she expelled from the rest of the match, she cannot play in her team's next match. In the next match her team can replace her such that her team can still play with all 11 players; only that particular player who received the red card cannot play. Relatedly, many soccer organizations such as state high school associations have rules limiting how many red cards a respective player can receive in a season. For example, a somewhat common rule is that if a player receives three red cards in one season, she is suspended from playing for the remainder of the season. Some high school associations also include a rule specifying if a player is suspended from the remainder of the soccer season due to obtaining a designated number of red cards, that player is also prohibited from playing in any other high school sports during the remainder of the school year.

Whereas red cards are issued for the most serious rule violations, yellow cards or *cautions* are issued for less serious yet still significant rule violations. Once a player receives a yellow card, she is cautioned about continuing that type of play but is allowed to continue playing the match. In some soccer associations, the player must leave the match at least momentarily. In the latter cases, the player receiving the yellow card can be replaced by a teammate such that her team does not have to play short a player. The player leaving the match due to the yellow card can re-enter the match at the next regular stoppage of play for which substitutions are allowed if her coach decides to send her back into the match.

Although yellow card violations are not as serious as red card violations in terms of detrimentally affecting a team's subsequent play, repeated yellow card violations by a respective player can be quite serious. If a player receives two yellow cards in one match, the result is essentially the same as receiving a red card: upon receiving the second yellow card, the player is prohibited from playing in the remainder of the match. Additionally, as with receiving a red card, the player's team cannot replace him on the field for the remainder of the soccer match. The player may also be suspended from playing in the next match, although not every soccer association requires suspension from the next match for two yellow card violations.

It should also be noted that coaches can be issued cards for specified rules violations, which usually involve a coach saying something that the referee considers unacceptable. The outcome of a coach receiving a card is similar to the outcomes just described for players receiving cards. In particular, if a coach receives a red card, he must leave the soccer field and general soccer area, and discontinue any coaching responsibilities for the remainder of the match. Spectators also can be penalized for engaging in activities interfering with the flow of a soccer match. Such activities usually involve ugly or otherwise highly inconsiderate yelling on the part of the spectators. In such occasions, spectators can be banned from watching the match, although this type of penalty does not occur very often. If spectators refuse to leave the viewing area, the referee can discontinue the match, which can subsequently result in the spectators' team having to forfeit the soccer match.

Hand Ball

A hand ball refers to a rule infraction in which a player (except the goal keeper within her team's penalty area) handles the ball with her *hand* or *arm*. Hand ball violations often cause confusion and/or disgruntlement for several reasons. First, the penalty for a hand ball is the awarding of a direct free kick to the opposing team. If the hand ball occurs within the defending team's penalty area, a *penalty kick* is awarded to the other team. As discussed earlier, penalty kicks represent excellent scoring opportunities for a team. Hence, the penalty for a hand ball can be quite severe for the team committing the violation.

A second reason hand ball violations often cause disgruntlement is that there is frequent misunderstanding about what actually constitutes a hand ball violation. Many spectators believe that a hand ball violation occurs any time a player touches the ball with his hand during field play. However, the definition of a hand ball is that the player carries, strikes or propels the ball with his hand or arm. Hence, a ball may inadvertently bounce and hit a player's hand without the player carrying, striking or propelling the ball himself. In the latter type of situation, a true hand ball has not occurred.

An additional reason hand balls cause confusion is that many referees are not particularly consistent in how they enforce the hand ball rule. Some referees call a hand ball essentially any time a player's hand touches the ball, regardless of the true definition. Consequently, spectators are rather likely to see inconsistency with enforcement of this rule across soccer matches; inconsistency that sets the occasion for disgruntlement among spectators, as well as players and coaches.

Official Definition Of A Hand Ball Violation
A player handles the ball—that is, a player carries, strikes, or propels the ball with a hand or arm.

Dangerous Play

The dangerous play rule requires considerable judgment on the part of the referee. In essence, a dangerous play call is made when the referee believes a player acted in a manner that was potentially or actually dangerous to himself or another player. A dangerous play results in the opposing team of the player who committed the play being awarded an indirect free kick. If the play is sufficiently dangerous in the opinion of the referee to be considered violent, then the play is considered a more serious rule infraction, resulting in a direct free kick. As alluded to earlier, the most serious (intentional) plays resulting in potential or actual harm to a player can result in a yellow or red card violation. However, the latter plays, due primarily to the apparent intentional aspect of the player's inappropriate action, are not considered dangerous plays per se but rather, violent conduct or serious foul play.

Common examples of dangerous play in many soccer matches involve *high kicks* and *playing the ball while a player is on the ground*. A high kick violation usually means a player kicked or attempted to kick a ball by bringing her leg high in the air while another player was in close proximity such that the latter player could be hurt by the kicking action. Playing the ball while a player is on the ground (e.g., kicking or attempting to kick the ball while lying down) is considered dangerous if another player is in close proximity. In the latter case, the player who is on the ground is often putting himself in a situation likely to cause physical harm by continuing to play the ball while other players are running around him.

Advantage

At times during most soccer matches, spectators will observe an obvious foul occur, such as a defensive player pushing the back of an opposing player who has control of the ball, without the referee whistling or stopping the play to call a foul—even though it seems apparent to spectators that the referee saw the foul occur. One legitimate reason for such a situation is that the referee did not call the foul because the offensive player had an *advantage* by continuing the ongoing play in contrast to having the play stopped and then re-started with a free kick. If the referee believes the team against which the foul was committed is better off or is likely to gain an *advantage* by continuing play—relative to stopping and then restarting play—the referee will adhere to the advantage rule and let the play continue. For example, a player might break away (Chapter 5) from the opposing defenders when a defender pushes or trips the player but the player does not lose her balance and continues the break away. In such a situation a referee would probably determine it was more advantageous for the player who was pushed or tripped to continue the break away rather than stopping the break away with a whistle and re-starting play.

Generally there are two ways spectators can determine if a referee evoked the advantage rule and did not whistle a foul when indeed a foul was committed (i.e., in contrast to the referee simply missing the foul and making a bad "no call"). First, the referee may use hand signals to indicate the players should continue playing. The appropriate signal in this regard is for the referee to push his hands and arms up and forward (with the hands facing palm up) toward the goal to which the player who was fouled is approaching. Sometimes referees will make this signal by motioning with only one hand and arm.

The second way to know a referee is evoking the advantage rule in contrast to simply missing the foul is when the referee yells *"play on"*. *Play on* is a verbal signal to the players that, in a situation in which a foul occurred, the referee is evoking the advantage call and that players should continue playing. Alternatively, a referee might instruct players to play on in a situation in which the referee expects players may think a foul was committed, but the referee does not believe that a foul actually occurred. In the latter situation, the referee is in essence informing the players not to stop play or to question the referee's judgment but to simply keep playing. At times a referee will signal the advantage ruling by simultaneously using the arm and hand signals along with the verbal signal of "play on".

Obstruction

Rule infractions regarding obstruction are not called very often by referees in youth soccer in the United States. However, the rule is mentioned here for two reasons. First, when it is called, many spectators are unaware as to what action on the field resulted in the referee blowing her whistle. Second, in a number of matches spectators will hear other spectators yell "obstruction" to the referee—usually meaning the latter spectators thought obstruction occurred and the referee did not call it. So spectators will know what is meant when obstruction is called, as well as have some idea as to when it should be called, the basic definition of obstruction is provided below.

Obstruction means a player used his body to block the path of an opposing player, without the former player making an apparent attempt to play the ball (**note:** obstruction is similar to the "pick" play in basketball in which a player physically blocks a player from guarding an opposing player). A common example is when the ball is about to roll out of the field of play and one player attempts to block another player from getting to the ball and keeping it on the playing field. The player who blocks the player's attempt to keep the ball on the field can do so only if the former player is also making a play on the ball. Otherwise, the former player is obstructing the opponent's play.

When obstruction is called by a referee, the opposing team (i.e., the team playing against the team which committed the foul) is typically awarded a free, indirect kick from the point at which the foul occurred. Alternatively, a direct kick can be awarded if the obstruction involved obvious and relatively intense physical contact with an opposing player.

Goals

It is typically quite obvious when a goal is scored, such that goals require little explanation for spectators. However, there are a few occasions when it is not so obvious when a goal is scored, usually resulting in a certain amount of confusion and displeasure among coaches, players and spectators. To avoid such confusion and disgruntlement, it helps to know what exactly constitutes a goal. For a goal to occur, the ball must pass *wholly* or *completely* across the goal line that extends between the two goal posts. The important point to remember is that the entire ball must cross the goal line.

Confusion arises as to whether a goal has been scored when the goal keeper stops the ball in the vicinity of the goal line and it is difficult to see if the ball completely crossed the goal line. In such cases it is the referee's judgment that determines if a goal was scored. At times it appears that a goal is scored because the keeper is standing inside the goal when she catches or otherwise stops the ball. It does not matter where the keeper is though, only whether the ball itself completely crossed the goal line. It also does not matter if the ball crosses the goal line and then immediately comes back out of the goal, such as when the ball bounces off one of the back uprights of the goal. Again, once the ball crosses the goal line between the goal posts and under the crossbar, a goal has been scored.

Confusion that frequently occurs when it is difficult to determine if a ball has crossed the goal line has, in part, given rise to a frequent cry in soccer: "put the ball in the *back of the net*". When the ball gets to the back of the net, a player has typically made a hard shot at the goal and there is no doubt the ball crossed the goal line.

For a goal to be scored, the entire ball must cross the goal line

Restarts

Restarts refer to certain actions that re-initiate field play that has been temporarily discontinued during an ongoing soccer match (or from a more technically correct standpoint in soccer terminology, *suspended*). Sometimes field play is temporarily stopped by the referee due to a rule infraction and then restarted with a free kick as described earlier in this chapter. More frequently, field play is interrupted by the ball going out of the field of play. The most common example of the latter interruption is due to the ball going outside either touch line, in which case field play is restarted with a throw-in as also discussed previously in this chapter. Less frequently, but nevertheless still common in essentially every soccer match, are temporary interruptions in ongoing field play due to the soccer ball going outside one of the goal lines at each end of the field (except of course if the ball crosses the goal line between the goal posts, in which case a goal is scored). When the ball crosses the goal line on either side of the goal, play is restarted with either a *goal kick* or *corner kick*, depending on which team last played, or touched, the ball prior to the ball leaving the field of play.

Goal kick. A goal kick is used to restart play when the ball is last touched by an offensive player before it crosses the goal line adjacent to the opponent's goal. The goal kick is then taken by the team defending the goal. From a spectator standpoint, there are three basic things to know about goal kicks. First, the kick can be taken from anywhere inside the *goal area* (see previous discussion in Chapter 2 regarding the goal area). Second, after the goal kick is taken, it cannot be touched by any player until the ball leaves the *penalty area* (again, see Chapter 2), either beyond the 18 line or beyond the outer side boundaries of the penalty area. Third, players on the opposing team from the player taking the goal kick cannot enter the kicking team's penalty area until the ball leaves the penalty area.

In most matches, the process of taking a goal kick is not controversial except for possible disagreement over which team last touched the ball prior to it going outside of the goal line. The latter situation can be controversial because if a referee mistake occurs and it is erroneously determined that a player on the team defending the goal last touched the ball, then a *corner kick* is awarded to the offensive team instead of a goal kick being awarded to the defending team. As explained below, corner kicks represent good scoring opportunities for the offensive team.

Corner kick. As just noted, corner kicks are used to restart field play when the ball goes out of play across the goal line after having been last touched by a player on the team defending the goal. Corner kicks are taken within the *corner area*, or *quarter circle*, at the corner of the field closest to the point at which the ball crossed the goal line. Key points to be aware of during corner kicks include the following: (a) a goal can be scored directly from a corner kick without touching any player, (b) players defending against the corner kick must be at least 10 yards away from the ball when it is kicked, and (c) offensive players—that is, players on the team that is taking the corner kick—do not have to be 10 yards away from the ball when it is kicked. The latter rule is important to note because sometimes a player taking the corner kick will restart play by kicking the ball to a teammate who is standing only a few feet from the spot at which the kick is taken. Implementing a corner kick in such a manner is usually part of a set play by the offensive team and is somewhat uncommon relative to how corner kicks are usually taken. The more common implementation strategy for taking a corner kick is for the player taking the kick to kick the ball in the air across the front of the goal with the intent that a teammate will then head or kick the ball into the goal.

In addition to the types of restarts just described, there is one other means of restarting field play that is relatively uncommon but still occurs occasionally. Specifically, sometimes a referee herself will restart play by a *drop ball* process. Drop balls are not discussed very often in the context of restarts because neither team has much control of the ball in such situations, typically disallowing set plays or immediate scoring opportunities. Drop balls are described in Chapter 7.

Substitutions

There are two general situations regarding player substitutions that often cause confusion among spectators. The first situation pertains to when, during the course of a soccer match, a player may be substituted for another player. For example, a parent may be eager for a son or daughter to enter a match and may not understand why the coach does not put the player in the match—even though it is clear the player is ready to enter and the coach plans to substitute the player (e.g., the player is standing on the side of the field loosening up, or waiting beside the coach). In such cases, the coach is usually waiting for an opportunity to send the player into the match in accordance with the rules; the coach can not simply substitute the player anytime she so desires.

Rules regarding when substitutions can be made vary according to different soccer associations and at times, according to age groups within associations. There is one rule however, that pertains to essentially all soccer matches: substitutions can only be made when there is a stoppage of field play. The most common times substitutions can be made during stoppages of play in youth soccer in the United States are summarized on the following page.

Allowable Times To Substitute Players in American Youth Soccer
  1. When play is stopped for a goal kick
  2. When a team is awarded a throw-in (only the team awarded the throw-in can substitute)
  3. When the opposing team substitutes for an injured player

In addition to the most common times when player substitutions are allowed as just summarized, there two other times when substitutions are allowed, and especially with older youth, such as with high school soccer teams. First, when a team is awarded a corner kick the team can then substitute players. Typically however, only the team awarded the corner kick can substitute; the opposing team can not substitute even though play is stopped for the corner kick. Second, when a player must leave the playing field temporarily due to having been issued a yellow card by the referee for a rule violation, another player can be substituted for that player. Again though, substitution rules vary across soccer associations and interested spectators should consult knowledgeable individuals about the substitution rules of their particular association.

The second situation causing frequent confusion in regard to substitutions pertains not to when the substitutions are allowed but rather, *how* the substitutions are made. At times a substitution is initiated but then stopped by the referee because, at least in the opinion of the referee, the substitution process did not follow the appropriate rules. Such incidents usually do not have much effect on the soccer match itself but nevertheless can cause confusion and some disgruntlement because the match is delayed and coaches, players and referees can become somewhat upset with the delays. Hence, it is helpful to know several key rules regarding how substitutions should be made. It should also be noted though, some of the confusion and disgruntlement results because various referees enforce substitutions differently such that what is allowed in one match is not allowed in another match.

The first rule regarding substitutions is that a player substitution can only occur during a stoppage in play on the field, such as during the times summarized earlier. Second, a substitution can only occur when the referee explicitly indicates a team may substitute a player. Generally, a coach or player must obtain the attention of the referee to indicate a desire to substitute (or alternatively, obtain the attention of a linesman who in turn obtains the attention of the referee on the field). Third, players entering the field to substitute for players must enter the field at the halfway-line. Fourth, the players entering the field must wait until the players leaving the field are entirely off the field before entering.

The latter two rules regarding substitutions are the ones most inconsistently enforced by referees. A rather common scenario is players become accustomed to referees in respective matches who let the players enter from anywhere on the field and then unexpectedly are prohibited from entering the field in this manner by a different referee in a subsequent soccer match. In the latter situation, the referee typically will stop the players as they are entering the field and make them go to the halfway-line and then enter the field.

Injuries

Although soccer is a relatively safe game compared to many other youth sports in the United States, as in essentially any competitive sport injuries do occur. It is the referee's judgment as to if and when a match should be temporarily stopped or suspended due to an injury. Such judgment often causes concern among spectators, due in part to the spectators' lack of familiarity with rules regarding stoppage of play due to injuries. For example, spectators or parents may notice that a player has been hurt and is lying on the ground, and become upset with the referee because she does not immediately stop play to allow assistance for the injured player. However, the rules require the referee to immediately stop play only if the referee observes a *serious* injury. If a referee observes that a player is only slightly injured, the rules call for the referee to wait to stop the match until the ball ceases to be in play (e.g., the ball goes outside of the field of play). Obviously, at times determining what constitutes a slight versus a serious injury requires some subjective judgment on the part of the referee—subjectivity that sets the occasion for disagreement among spectators.

Soccer Uniforms and Equipment

From a spectator standpoint, soccer uniforms and equipment typically do not evoke much enthusiasm or concern during a match. There are several rules though that occasionally are not adhered to by players, such that a referee will stop an ongoing match to correct the situation. When a match is temporarily suspended due to a uniform or equipment rules violation, the offending player can be sent off the field to correct the situation. So that spectators will know what the points of concern are when there is stoppage of play, or a respective player has to leave the field of play due to an inappropriate uniform or equipment, the most common rules that are violated by players are listed below.

Common Rules Pertaining To Soccer Uniforms And Equipment
1. Players must have their shirts tucked in their shorts or pants
2. Players must wear shin guards
3. Players must not wear items likely to cause harm to themselves or others
4. Goal keepers must wear colors that distinguish them from other players and the referee

---

At first glance, the rules regarding clothing and equipment seem somewhat unimportant or superficial. However, there are legitimate reasons for the rules. For example, with rule 1 above, having the shirts tucked in makes it more difficult for players to illegally hold an opposing player by grabbing his shirt. For rule 2, shin guards are required for protection for players. Likewise, rule 3, which generally refers to loose jewelry that can cut or scratch (e.g., ear rings and watches), is for player protection. Rule 4 pertaining to the color of the goal keeper's jersey is designed to facilitate the players' and referee's job in terms of knowing when the keeper is playing the ball versus when a field player is playing the ball. The latter issue is important when there are groups of players around the ball in front of the goal and it can be difficult to distinguish one player from another.

The degree to which the rules just summarized are enforced vary noticeably across matches and referees. Not all the rules are required by some soccer associations, and in particular, not all associations require players to wear shin guards. Likewise, not all referees consistently enforce the rule about players keeping their shirts or jerseys inside their soccer shorts. The rules are gradually becoming more commonplace in soccer in the United States though, and referees have begun to enforce the rules more stringently.

Section 2

Common Soccer Terms
And Phrases

Heard During Soccer Matches

Chapter 5

COMMON SOCCER TERMS AND PHRASES USED WITH THE OFFENSE

This chapter provides explanations of soccer terms and phrases frequently heard during a soccer match. The terms and phrases are used by coaches and players to communicate game strategy and general direction, as well as in commendation and criticism for certain actions of respective players. Familiarity with the terminology to be presented in this and subsequent chapters can significantly enhance a soccer spectator's understanding and enjoyment of the game of soccer.

The terms and phrases summarized in the remainder of this chapter are most frequently used in regard to offensive play; play aimed at getting shots at the goal, and getting the ball in the goal. Chapter 6 summarizes terminology most frequently used in regard to defensive play. For organizational purposes, the terms and phrases are simply presented in alphabetical order. Where more than one term or phrase is used to mean essentially the same thing, the terms and phrases are presented together with the less frequently used terms and phrases following the most frequently used ones. However, the differentiation regarding frequency of use is sometimes rather irrelevant because the descriptors may be used interchangeably by different coaches or players.

Back (got me back; drop; got a drop)

A player without the ball is unguarded by an opposing

player and is behind a teammate who has control of the ball, and instructs the player with the ball that she has the option of passing the ball *back,* or *dropping* the ball, to the unguarded player. The declaration is usually provided because the player with the ball may not see, or otherwise be unaware, that her teammate is in a position behind her to receive a pass.

Breakaway

A play in which a player has the ball by himself past all opposing defensive players (except the keeper) and is in a foot race to stay ahead of the pursuing defenders in a run to the goal; the player has *broken away* from the defensive players. A breakaway usually results in an individual confrontation between the player with the ball and the opposing goal keeper.

Carry (dribble)

A reference for a player who has control of the ball to maintain control herself and to advance the ball forward with the feet—to *carry* the ball herself in contrast to passing the ball to a teammate. The instruction to carry is usually given when a coach or player sees that her teammate has the ball without any opposing players in close proximity. The intent is to let the teammate know she has room to advance the ball herself without interference from opposing players. Carrying is alternatively referred to as *dribbling* similar to dribbling a ball with the hands in basketball except that the movement of the ball is of course made by contact with the feet.

Change fields (change it; switch fields; switch it)

An instruction to kick a long pass to the other side of the field—that is, *change* the side of the field on which the ball is played. The intended purpose is for the player to kick the ball far across the field to the left or right side, or at an angle to the right or left front. The intent is to move the offensive play forward to an unguarded player across the width of the field, because most or all of the defensive players have shifted to the side of the field where the ball is currently positioned.

Control (possession)

A general direction to better control the ball with relatively short, accurate passes from player to (unguarded) player. This instruction, commonly heard from coaches of younger and less experienced players, often occurs when the players tend to kick the ball rather wildly or attempt to kick the ball long distances without apparent concern for getting the ball in a controlled fashion to an unguarded teammate. The intent in part is for one team to control the ball, or maintain *possession* of the ball, and keep it away from the opposing players while the former team maneuvers for a shot on goal.

Cross it (center; center it; serve it; service)

A player has the ball in the corner area of the field adjacent to the opposition's goal and is instructed to kick the ball across the field, parallel to the goal. In this manner, the player is instructed to *cross* the ball in front of the *center* of the goal. The intent is for a teammate to receive the ball as it crosses the front of the goal and put the ball in the goal. As such, the player who kicks the ball is *serving* the ball to his teammate in order for the latter player to receive the ball and make a shot toward the goal.

Far post (back post)

An instruction for a player to kick the ball toward the side of the opponent's goal farthest away from the player—which is just inside the far goal post (one of the two posts extending from the ground to support the cross bar on the goal). Conversely, *near post* refers to kicking the ball to the side of the goal that is nearest the player. The instruction is typically given when a coach or player believes the most advantageous place to get the ball in the goal is just inside the far or near post, respectively.

Finish (finish it)

A declaration to shoot the ball in the net. The instruction usually occurs when offensive players have made one or several nice plays to put their team in a good position to score a goal. The instruction is then given to *finish* the play by achieving the ultimate outcome of the play of scoring a goal. Relatedly, following a soccer match reference is often heard, or read in the newspaper's account of the match, about a team that was unable to finish. The latter reference means a team had opportunities to score but did not score—the team did not *finish* the offensive plays. Often such a reference is used to describe team play in which the team took a lot of shots on goal but did not actually score goals with the shots due to either repeatedly missing the goal or being stopped by the opposing team's goal keeper.

First time (one touch)

A directive to a player to play the ball (e.g., with the foot or head) as soon as the ball comes to the player, usually meaning to quickly pass or shoot the ball. In this manner the player advances the ball the *first time* she touches it, in contrast to gaining control of the ball and then advancing it. In the latter situation, the player must touch the ball several times whereas with a *first time* play, *one touch* on the ball is all that is made by the player. The directive is usually given when a coach or teammate believes a player does not have time to touch the ball more than one time in order to advance it without interference from an opposing player.

Get in the box (in the box)

An instruction to a player who has control of the ball relatively near the opposing team's goal to advance the ball to within the penalty box. The rationale is generally two-fold: (1) typically the easiest area from which to shoot the ball in the goal is right in front of the goal, which is the area included within the penalty box and, (2) if a *major* foul is committed by a defensive player against an offensive player in the penalty box, the infraction results in a penalty kick. In contrast, a major foul outside the penalty box results in a direct kick but not a penalty kick. As indicated in Chapter 4, penalty kicks usually represent excellent opportunities for a team to score a goal.

Give it up (give it)

An instruction to a player who has control of the ball to pass the ball to a teammate. Frequently this instruction is provided by a coach or another player who believes the player who has the ball is dribbling too much with too many opposing players around such that she runs the risk of losing control of the ball to the other team.

Go to goal

An instruction to a player who has control of the ball to maintain control and to advance the ball himself directly to the goal. The instruction is usually given when a coach or player sees that a teammate is in a position, typically on the opposing team's half of the field, to carry (see *carry* earlier in this chapter) the ball himself straight toward the goal without the likelihood of interference from opposing players. The intent is to alert the player not to be concerned with looking to pass the ball to a teammate, but to get in a position to shoot on goal himself.

Have one

An instruction—usually a very quick instruction—for a

player to immediately shoot the ball at the goal.

Head up

A directive to a player who is dribbling the ball to pick her *head up* such that she can see around the field. The directive is typically given to younger and less skilled players who tend to look at their feet and the ball while dribbling. In the latter situation, the player has her head pointed down and can not see what her teammates are doing and hence, can not pass the ball very well to a teammate who is in the best position to receive a pass.

High ball (long ball; boot it)

A directive to kick the ball high and far. The purpose is usually to kick the ball over the opposing midfielders and defensive players to a speedy forward. Such a play can result in a break away for the forward, representing a good opportunity to get a shot on goal (see also *send it* later in this chapter).

In the air (win it in the air; win it)

A command for a player or players to reach the ball while the ball is in the air before it hits the ground and before an opposing team player reaches the ball. The directive is often given when a teammate or opposing player is taking a long kick, such as a goal keeper's punt or a goal kick, which usually results in the ball being sent high in the air. The directive is also commonly given when an opposing team is usually getting to balls in the air before one's own team. The intent is to encourage one's own players to beat the other team to the ball—to *win* the ball in contrast to losing the ball to an opposing player—before it reaches the ground.

Look at ..."player's name"

An instruction for a player who has control of the ball to get the ball to the named player. The instruction may be given during the ongoing action of the game, or when play is being restarted by a free kick.

Make a run

A directive to a player who does not have the ball to *run* up the field in open *space* (see *space* later in this chapter) in order to be in a position to receive a pass from a teammate and advance the ball toward the goal. Generally, the directive is given when a player or coach sees there is an open area on the field with no opposing players and if the player to whom the directive is given quickly gets to that area, he will be in an advantageous position to receive a pass from his teammate.

Man on (man coming; on your back)

An exclamation to a player who has the ball that an opposing player is approaching him, typically from behind, or in *back* of, the player with the ball. The statement is usually made because it appears the player with the ball does not see the approaching opponent. The intent is to instruct the player to pass the ball to a teammate before the opposing player reaches him from behind, and possibly takes away control of the ball.

Move to space (space, movement, running off the ball)

A directive to one or more players who do not have the ball to move to a part of the field where there are no opposing players—that is, to open *space*. The intent is to position players in different parts on the field to allow the player who has the ball to advance it by passing to an unguarded teammate. The directive is usually heard most frequently in matches involving younger or less experienced players who have a tendency to go wherever the ball is, resulting in crowding or *bunching up* around the ball with no appreciable space between the players.

On sides (get on)

A directive for a player, usually a forward, who does not have the ball and is in an off sides position (Chapter 4) to move to an on sides position. To respond to the directive, the player must either back up away from the opposing team's goal to a position even with the opposing team's last defender (excluding the keeper) or to move back past the halfway-line. Often this directive is given as a reminder to a forward not to be caught in an off sides position when a teammate passes her the ball.

One v one (beat him; take him)

An instruction to a player who has control of the ball that he is in a situation in which he has only one opposing player to get the ball past in order to get a shot toward the goal, or to set up a teammate for a goal shot. In this manner, the player is instructed that he should work to get past, or *beat*, the defending player. The instruction further directs the player with the ball to advance it solely himself past the opposing player.

Overlap

An instruction to a player who does not have the ball, and is in a position close to and behind a teammate who has the ball, to run past or *overlap* the player who has the ball. The basic idea is when the player without the ball runs by her teammate who has the ball, the former player will be in an open or unguarded position to receive a pass from the latter player. A common variation is for a player with the ball to pass it ahead to a teammate, run by (again, *overlap*) the teammate and then

SOCCER MADE SIMPLE

receive a pass back from the teammate. The latter type of play is often referred to as a *give and go* (similar to a "give and go" play in basketball); the player with the ball passes, or *gives*, the ball to a teammate and then runs, or *goes*, past the player to receive the ball back. The "give and go" is also referred to as a *triangle* because the movement of the ball from the player who originally has the ball to another player and then back to the former player forms a triangle.

Pressure (keep the pressure on)

From an offensive perspective (see Chapter 6 for reference to *pressure* from a defensive standpoint), pressure refers to continuously taking shots toward the goal. The intent is to put *pressure* on the goal keeper and defenders by repeatedly shooting the ball. The directive is usually given when a team is frequently getting the ball close to the opposition's goal.

Send it (send ... "player's name")

A directive to a player with the ball to kick a long pass in the air past all opposing players and one's own teammates. The intent is to *send* the ball past the opposing players and let the teammate, often a forward, chase the ball down by outrunning the opposing players and get a shot on goal. A directive to send a player (e.g., "*send Debi!*") means to kick the ball over one particular player for her to run the ball down past the defenders.

Settle (settle it)

Settle refers to gaining control of the ball, usually by slowing the movement of the ball, or placing the ball with the feet on the ground. In this way, the ball is *settled* from the air to the ground. This directive is typically given when a team is kicking a lot of balls in the air, which are usually more difficult for teammates to control than balls kicked on the ground, or otherwise not maintaining good control of the ball.

Shield

A directive to a player who has control of the ball to position herself such that her body is between the ball and an opposing player who is attempting to take the ball away from her. By putting her body between the opposing player and the ball, the player is *shielding* the ball from the opposing player, thereby making it more difficult for the opposing player to take the ball away from her.

Shot

This popular instruction usually does not cause much confusion; a player appears open to take a shot and should, at least in the mind of the player or coach who yells *shot*, immediately shoot the ball at the goal. Other common variations include *shoot, take it, take one, rip it,* and *pull the trigger* (see also *have one* described earlier in this chapter).

Square

A directive typically provided by a player without the ball who is on a horizontal line with a teammate who has the ball (i.e., a line extending perpendicular from the player with the ball who is facing toward the goal; the square line goes toward the touch line). The directive informs the player with the ball that he can pass the ball to an unguarded player by kicking the ball straight toward the touch line on the side where the player shouts the instruction.

Support (show; show for it; move to him)

An instruction to one or more players who do not have the ball to move to an open space closer to their teammate who has the ball. The directive is usually given when it appears the player with the ball is in danger of losing the ball to the opposing team. By moving closer to the teammate with the ball, the players are *supporting,* or *helping,* the teammate by giving the teammate the option of passing the ball to another player. A call for support is sometimes made by calling for *help* (see Chapter 6 for help as it refers to defensive play). Alternatively, instructing to *show for it* means essentially for a player to move closer to his teammate, and within the teammate's field of vision, to *show* his teammate that he is open to receive a pass.

Talk

An instruction to players to verbally inform each other about what is happening on the field. The intent is to increase *talking* between and among players so that they can better control the flow of the game through communication. More specifically, the instruction is intended to get players to tell their teammates about what they cannot immediately see occurring. By continuously talking to teammates in this manner, players are less likely to unexpectedly lose control of the ball due to an unseen opposing player taking the ball away. Further, by frequently talking to each other, players are more likely to be aware of open teammates to pass to, as well as chances to immediately take opportune shots. In essence, the purpose is to get players to use the directives and instructions presented in this and the subsequent chapter to improve their awareness of options for controlling the overall flow of the game.

Through

A directive for a player who has the ball to pass the ball *on the ground through,* or between, defensive players directly to or in front of a teammate who is in a position to run the ball down in front of the goal and take a shot on goal. The directive is typically issued when the player with the ball is in the middle of the field somewhere close to the 18 (see Chapter 3 for elaboration on the 18).

Time

A statement to a player who is receiving the ball from a teammate that there are no opposing players close by such that the player has *time* to decide what to do with the ball (i.e., in contrast to having to immediately send the ball to a teammate due to being closely guarded by an opposing player who is likely to take the ball away). This statement is delivered both to offensive players and to defensive players. In the case of offensive players, the statement is intended to inform the player receiving the ball she has time to set up an offensive play. In the case of defensive players, the statement informs the player receiving the ball she does not have to immediately *clear* (Chapter 6) the ball away from her own goal.

Turn

An instruction for a player who has just received the ball to *turn* around with the ball. The instruction is typically given when a player is facing away from his goal in order to receive a pass from a teammate such that his back is to his own goal. The intent is to inform the player there is not an opposing player immediately behind him such that he has time to turn around and then advance the ball himself or pass to a teammate without immediate interference from an opposing player.

Volley

Volley refers to kicking the ball before the ball hits the ground (that is, to kick the ball when the ball is in the air). An instruction to volley generally means a player should shoot the ball at the goal by getting her foot on the ball when it is coming to her in the air. The intent is that by kicking the ball before it hits the ground, the player can get a shot off more quickly than if she waits for the ball to hit the ground. By getting the ball shot quickly, the player is less likely to have opposing players interfere with the shot.

What do you see (see what you have)

An instruction to a player who has the ball to quickly look and *see* where her teammates are in order to set up an offensive play involving one or more teammates.

Wide (go wide)

An instruction for a player to pass the ball to the outside, or *wide*, part of the field, often to a wing or outside midfielder. The instruction may also be given to direct a player, usually a wing, to position himself on the outside part of the field in order to subsequently receive a pass. The instruction is often given when a team is tending to keep the ball in the middle of the field and there are too many opposing players in the middle portion of the field to allow the team to maintain control of the ball.

You're standing

A declaration, usually from a coach, that players are *standing still* and not moving around the field in order to establish an effective offense. The intent is the same as when a coach instructs players to *move to space*, or yells *movement* or *space* as described earlier in this chapter.

Chapter 6

COMMON SOCCER TERMS AND PHRASES USED WITH THE DEFENSE

This chapter continues the process initiated in Chapter 5 of explaining common terms and phrases used during soccer matches in the United States. Whereas Chapter 5 presented terminology pertaining to offensive plays though, this chapter discusses terms and phrases related to the defensive aspects of soccer—those components of team play designed to prevent the opposing team from getting shots on goal and from scoring goals. As in Chapter 5, the soccer terms and phrases are listed in alphabetical order. Where there is more than one term or phrase used to convey essentially the same meaning, the most commonly used term or phrase is presented first, followed by the less commonly used terms or phrases. As also noted in Chapter 5 however, many of the terms to be presented are used interchangeably.

Back door (back side)

An instruction to a defensive player who is positioned close to her goal that an opposing offensive player is unguarded in *back* of her close to the goal on the opposite side of the field (width wise) from where another offensive player has the ball. The instruction is intended to warn the defensive player that the opposition may attempt to "sneak in the *back door*" to get in position behind the defender to receive a pass for a shot on goal in contrast to "coming in the *front door*" (i.e., taking a shot from where the ball is currently on the field in front of the defensive player). *Back door* alerts the defense to guard the open player on the opposite or *back* side of the field away from the ball.

Challenge (challenge her)

An instruction for a player to approach an opponent who has control of the ball and attempt to disrupt, or *challenge*, the opponent's play or take the ball away from her. The instruction is often given when an opponent has the ball in an unguarded position and no defensive player appears to be attempting to move to the opponent who has the ball. The intent is to instruct a defensive player to approach the opponent and disallow her time to create an offensive play.

Clear (clear it)

A directive to immediately kick the ball far away from one's own goal. The purpose is to alert defensive players to quickly *clear* the ball away from the area in front of the goal. The directive is typically given when the opposing team has one or several offensive players close to the goal with a high probability of getting a good shot on goal.

Contain

An instruction to a defensive player to guard an opposing player who has the ball by keeping, or *containing*, the latter player in a certain area of the field. The intent is to instruct the defensive player not to make an aggressive play by trying to get the ball away from the opposing player (see *tackle* later in this chapter) and risk letting the latter player get by the defensive player. In short, the purpose is to prevent the opposing player from advancing the ball herself toward the goal. By containing the offensive player in this manner, the defensive player is in essence "buying time" for her defensive teammates to come over and help defend the goal.

Drop back (help; help out)

An instruction, frequently given to a specific player, to move *back* toward his own goal in order to better defend the goal. The instruction is typically provided when a coach or teammate observes that there are unguarded opposing players close to the player's goal, or that the offensive players are mounting an attack (Chapter 7) on goal and soon will have more players close to the goal relative to the existing number of defensive players who are in a position to defend the goal. By dropping back toward one's own goal, a player can help ensure his team has sufficient players close to the goal to prevent the opposing team from having unguarded players in a position to take a shot on goal. An alternative, though much less frequently used instruction, to *drop back* is sometimes given by defensive players by instructing to *help out* or simply, *help*.

Goalside (get goalside)

An instruction for one or more defensive players to guard a respective offensive player who is in a position to receive the ball from a teammate by standing close to the player and between the offensive player and the goal the defenders are protecting. In this manner the defensive players position themselves on the *side* of the offensive player that is closest to the *goal*. By being on the goal side of the offensive player, the defensive player makes it more difficult for the offensive opponent to get a good shot on goal or otherwise advance the ball to the goal.

Mark up (mark)

A directive to closely guard an opposing player who does

not have the ball in order to prevent the player from receiving a pass and getting an easy shot on goal. Marking generally involves a defensive player standing right next to the offensive player who is to be marked and between the offensive player and the goal—that is, *goalside*. The directive is usually given when the opposition has the ball close to a team's goal, and particularly when there is a re-start close to the goal such as for example, a corner kick or an indirect kick inside the penalty box. In the latter situation, the intent is that every offensive player will be closely guarded or *marked* by a defensive player.

No turn

An instruction to a defensive player to closely guard an opposing player who has just received the ball, or is about to receive the ball, in order to prevent the opposing player from *turning* around with the ball to be in a position to face the player's goal. Typically this instruction occurs in a situation in which an opposing player has his back to the defensive player in order to receive a pass from a teammate who is behind him (see *turn* in Chapter 5). The intent is also to disallow the opposing player from turning toward the goal in order to see what type of offensive opportunity exists by advancing the ball toward the goal.

Numbers (they have numbers)

A declaration that there are more opposing offensive players close to the goal than defensive players. The purpose of the declaration is to alert one's team that more players are needed to *drop back* as described previously in this chapter and help defend against the offensive players. By having *numbers*, an opposing offensive team has an advantage over the defenders because when there is a larger number of offensive players than defensive players close to the goal, the defenders cannot closely guard each offensive player (hence, at least one offensive player could be quite open or unguarded to take a shot on goal).

Off (off sides, she's off)

A declaration, typically made by a player or coach (or spectator), that an opposing player is in an off sides position during an ongoing play. The purpose is usually to alert the referee that an opposing player is in an off sides position. The referee, of course, may or may not respond to the declaration in terms of calling an off-sides violation against the opposing player.

Play it like a corner

A directive that defensive players should line up in positions as if they were defending a *corner kick* (Chapter 7). The usual defensive line-up for a corner kick is for the defensive players to guard or *mark* each offensive player closely by staying between the offensive player and the goal. The directive is typically given when the opposing team is taking a throw-in close to the defenders' goal and whoever yells the directive believes the player taking the throw-in can make a long throw to the goal, with the ball approaching the goal as it typically does during a corner kick.

Pressure (pressure him)

An instruction to a player to approach and closely guard and/or attempt to tackle (see *tackle* later in this chapter) an opposing player who has the ball. The instruction to pressure usually is given when an opposing player has the ball close to his own goal or in the midfield area. The intent is that if the player on defense can *pressure* the opposing player into making a mistake and giving up the ball, then the defensive player's team can take control of the ball in good offensive position to set up a shot on goal. The instruction to *pressure* is very similar to the instruction to *challenge* as described earlier in this chapter.

Push up

A directive for the last line of defensive players to move up, or *push* up, the field away from their own goal. The purpose is to disallow the opposing offensive players from being close to one's goal. When the defensive players push up away from their own goal, the offensive players cannot stay close to the goal because they would be in an off sides position. The directive is also given to direct the defensive players to move up the field such that they will be in a position to obtain the ball closer to the opponent's goal. The directive is frequently provided with the latter intent when the defensive players are tending to continuously position themselves close to their own goal to prevent scoring opportunities by the other team. Such a situation often occurs with younger or inexperienced defensive players who think they should always stay close to their own goal. Similarly, the situation frequently occurs with more experienced players when the opposing team is tending to maintain possession of the ball and is getting a lot of shots on goal—a situation that can cause defensive players to forget about their overall responsibilities across the entire field in terms of helping set up the offense, and to become anxiously concerned about only defending their goal.

Save

Save refers to a play made by the goal keeper in which the keeper stops a shot on goal from going into the net and hence, *saves* a goal from being scored. Typically a save involves a keeper catching or otherwise playing the ball with his hands. However, the keeper can use any part of his body (e.g., by sliding toward the ball and kicking or blocking it with his feet) to stop the ball from going into the goal. Sometimes, when the keeper prevents a goal in the latter manner, the play is referred to as a *stop* in contrast to a save (i.e., the keeper *stops* the ball from entering the goal).

Shadow (shadow her)

A directive for a player to guard an opposing player who has the ball by staying close to the player but not letting the player get by her. The defensive player follows, or *shadows*, the offensive player's moves but does not make an aggressive attempt to actually take the ball away from the offensive player. In this manner the defensive player plays a cautious type of defense by keeping the offensive player from advancing the ball toward the goal but not an aggressive type of defense in terms of trying to take the ball away. The latter type of play is more aggressive but also riskier in terms of increasing the likelihood of the offensive player getting by the defensive player. *Shadowing* serves essentially the same purpose as *containing*, as described earlier.

Step up

On a general level, *step up* means for defensive players to move up the field a few steps away from their own goal. However, *step up* can also refer to two specific ways to move up the field, depending on the situation. In one situation, usually when the ball is on the defending team's side of the halfway-line and the team with the ball is likely to be making passes, *step up* means for the back line of defenders to move up the field a few steps to put the opposing team's forwards in an off sides position. By stepping up in this manner, which is essentially the same as *pushing up* as described earlier, the defenders can legally disallow the opposing team's forwards from receiving a pass (i.e., because the forwards would then be in an offsides position). In the other typical situation in which *step up* is instructed, the intent is for a defensive player to: (1) move up immediately next to an opposing player who is about to receive a pass, frequently in a position with her back to the defensive player, or has just received a pass, and (2) disallow the opposing player's control of the ball by tackling or otherwise getting her own foot on the ball. With the latter type of *step up* instruction the intent is really to step up next to a specific opposing player whereas with the former *step up* instruction, the intent is to step up the field in general.

Stick

A directive for a player to approach an opposing player who has control of the ball in a relatively still position and to establish himself immediately next to the player to kick the ball away from the opposing player's feet. Such a play typically occurs when the defensive player uses his body to physically pressure the opposing player from behind without overtly pushing the player and *sticks* the ball with his foot. The directive is also given in terms of the defender *sticking* the opposing player himself with his body, although the true intent is to hit the ball away from the player's feet.

Tackle

Tackle instructs a defensive player to use his feet to take the ball away from an opposing player who is *carrying* or *dribbling* the ball (Chapter 5). One specific type of tackle is a *slide tackle*. In a slide tackle, the defensive player slides on the ground with his body and takes the ball away by kicking it with his foot while sliding. Slide tackles typically are not seen very often however, for three reasons. First, slide tackles are more likely to result in injury to either the defensive player who is sliding or the offensive player who has the ball relative to tackling from a standing position. Second, by sliding, the defensive player is making a more risky play because if he misses the ball and is lying on the ground, he is less able to recover quickly and stop the offensive player relative to if he misses the ball from a standing position. Finally, sliding into a ball is more likely to result in a foul because the player has less body control while sliding on the ground and may slide into the opposing player rather than into the ball. Sliding into a player represents a rule infraction or foul.

Turn wide (turn her wide)

An instruction to a player who has the ball on the defensive end of the field (i.e., closer to her team's goal than to the opposing team's goal) to take the ball to the outside or *wide* part of the field. The instruction is typically given when the player is being challenged, or about to be challenged, by an opposing player. By instructing the defensive player to take, or *turn*, the ball to the wide part of the field, the player is informed she is about to be challenged and if indeed the challenge is successful and the player gives up the ball to the opposing team in the wide part of the field, at least the opposing team will get the ball in a position away from the goal. Alternatively, if the defensive player keeps the ball in the middle portion of the field and loses the ball to the opposing team, the opposing team will be in a good position to get a shot on goal. In a similar manner, the instruction to *turn her wide* refers to a defensive player making an opposing offensive player who has control of the ball move to the wide part of the field (i.e., in contrast to allowing the offensive player to move the ball in the middle part of the field, which is more likely to result in a good shot on goal).

Wall (form a wall; make a wall)

A directive, issued when the opposing team has been awarded a free kick close to one's goal, for several players to stand side by side between the goal and the opposing player who will be taking the kick toward the goal. The intent is for the players to form a human *wall* between the kicker and the goal, thereby interfering with the kicker's shot on goal. The number of players forming the wall varies depending primarily on how close the ball is to the goal, with larger number of players forming the wall when the ball will be kicked from a spot close to the goal. Typically the defending goal keeper determines how many players should form the wall by shouting "3" for 3 players in the wall, "4" for 4 players, etc.

Chapter 7

MISCELLANEOUS TERMS COMMONLY HEARD DURING SOCCER MATCHES

This chapter presents common terms and phrases heard during soccer matches in the United States that do not readily fall within the chapter topics previously covered. The most popular of these terms and phrases usually involve commendations and praise for laudable soccer play. Other terms and phrases are presented that are not used primarily with offensive or defensive plays as is the terminology presented in the two preceding chapters, respectively. However, the terms and phrases are still common to the game of soccer from an overall standpoint.

Popular Commendations Unique to Soccer

The meaning of many of the soccer terms and phrases presented in this section is often readily apparent when heard by spectators during soccer matches. Each of the terms and phrases is used to refer to a particular play by one or more soccer players, or to the overall play of a soccer team, that is viewed as commendable. However, the terminology is presented here because the terms and phrases are rather unique to the game of soccer. The uniqueness is due in large part to the fact that the terms and phrases often have their origin in terminology associated with soccer played in other countries. The terminology has been adopted within soccer circles in the United States due primarily to the influence of soccer coaches who have come to the United States from abroad and continue to use terminology with which they were accustomed in their home countries. Subsequently, their terminology has been adopted by American players and coaches, and to an increasing degree recently, American soccer spectators.

Following the organizational format utilized in preceding chapters, the popular commendations unique to soccer are listed in alphabetical order with an accompanying explanation as to the specific meaning of the commendation.

Good ball

This commendation is heard frequently during many soccer matches. Most commonly, the commendation refers to a player who made a very nice pass, and usually a relatively long pass, to set up a teammate in an opportune position to make a strong offensive play such as getting a good shot on goal. The *good* aspect can refer either to the effectiveness in placing the ball in a strategic location with the pass, or to the apparent knowledge of the player as to knowing where to send the ball.

It'll come

This phrase is typically offered as encouragement to a team or specific players to keep doing what they are doing. The statement frequently is heard when a team is getting in position for good shots on goal but are not actually scoring goals due, for example, to outstanding goal keeper play by the opposing team. Generally, the phrase is intended to imply if the designated players keep playing the way they have been playing a goal (*it*) eventually *will come* from the play.

Nice idea (good idea)

A commendation typically offered when a player attempts

to make a play viewed as reflecting good knowledge as to what should be done to help the player's team but the play was not completed successfully. For example, a left midfielder may see that a teammate is unguarded way across the other side of the field and the midfielder attempts to send a long pass to the player (see *change it* in Chapter 5) but the receiving player misses the ball and the ball goes outside the touch line or to an opposing player. In such a case another player or coach may offer commendation or encouragement to the player who sent the pass because she did the right thing even though the play was unsuccessful.

Unlucky

This declaration is very similar to *nice idea* presented above. The descriptor is generally heard when a player makes a good play that did not quite reach success, and often due to factors out of the respective player's control. To illustrate, a player may send a long lead pass to a teammate down the wide side of the field adjacent to the touch line that puts the teammate in an opportune position to readily advance the ball to the goal but due to a bad bounce or a sloping field, the ball rolls out of the field of play before the teammate can catch up to it. In this manner, the player made a nice play with the pass but due in essence to *bad luck* the play was not completed as desired. The statement frequently is given to offer encouragement to the player to keep up the good play and not to let the bad luck discourage his play.

Well done

This phrase is rather self-explanatory, representing commendation for essentially any type of play that a coach or player views as praiseworthy. The phrase is mentioned here because it is heard very frequently in soccer matches whereas it is not a very common praise statement in other American sports. Other phrases used to offer general commendation for desirable play that are relatively unique to soccer and not frequently used in other popular sports in the United States include *good stuff* and *great stuff.*

General Soccer Terms and Phrases
Heard During Matches

As noted earlier in this chapter, there are some terms and phrases heard frequently during soccer matches in the United States that do not fall neatly into offensive or defensive situations, and are not used for commendation for good soccer play. This chapter section presents the most popular of these types of miscellaneous terminology.

Added time

The official timing of the duration of a soccer match is never stopped through time outs as it is in other popular American sports such as basketball and football. In short, the time allotted to play a soccer match (e.g., 40 minutes per half in most high school soccer associations) is never stopped by a referee. However, certain stoppages of play, or suspension of play, such as when yellow or red cards are issued or when there is an injury to a player that requires a relatively considerable amount of time to attend to on the field, result in what is considered *added time.* Adding time involves the amount of time encompassed by the stoppage in play being added to the amount of designated time for playing the respective half of the match in which the stoppage occurred. Such a situation can be confusing to spectators because if the timing of a match is shown on a scoreboard (usually a football scoreboard) and the time runs out, play frequently continues on the field. In the latter cases, the referee has added time to the half and play will continue throughout the amount of time the referee has added to the match. In this regard, in soccer the official time is always maintained by the referee on the field, regardless of whether time is represented on a scoreboard clock. In order to alert spectators that the official time is maintained by the referee on the field and not on the scoreboard, many associations stop the scoreboard time when there are only a few minutes left in the match. In this manner, when the scoreboard clock stops spectators are informed that there is not much time left in the match and that the referee will signal when the time is complete.

Assist

An *assist* refers to a play in which a player passes the ball to a teammate and the teammate immediately scores a goal. In this manner, the player has *assisted* her teammate who gets credit for the goal. The term *assist* is taken in part from American hockey and basketball and is a term more commonly used in the United States relative to other countries in which soccer is played.

Attacking

Attacking refers to a style of play in which a team places an apparent emphasis on offense and getting a lot of shots on goals—the team continuously *attacks* its opponent's goal. Similarly, *mounting an attack* refers to a particular play or series of plays in which a team begins to put itself in a position to get shots on goal by controlling movement of the ball far away from the opponent's goal, and working the ball closer to the goal in a controlled fashion with the eventual outcome of getting a good shot on goal. Related to attacking is a *counter attack*. A counter attack refers to a play in which a team that is in a position of defending its goal, or defending against an attack on its goal, quickly gains control of the ball and immediately advances the ball to the opposing team's goal in an offensive manner. In this way, the team *counters* the opposition's offensive play by quickly *attacking* the goal itself. Counter attacks often represent a good opportunity to score because the opposing team, after having missed an opportunity to score a goal itself during an offensive play, can be caught off guard as the other team quickly takes the ball back down the field.

Bend it

An instruction to a player about to take a free kick to send the ball in a manner that the ball curves or *bends* while in the air. Typically, the intent is to instruct the player to *bend* the flight of the ball around a wall (Chapter 6) of opposing players who are attempting to block the shot from getting to the goal. A ball that is successfully bent in this manner is sometimes referred to as a banana because the flight of the ball resembles the shape of a banana. However, it should be noted considerable skill is required to curve a ball in flight in a specific manner, and most youth soccer players do not posses this skill. Actually, a kick that results in a ball curving while in flight is usually done unintentionally by players due to somewhat inadequate kicking skills.

Bicycle

A *bicycle* refers to a type of kick in which a player kicks the ball in a direction behind her by meeting the ball in the air with her foot and swinging her foot over her head while throwing her body in the air horizontal with the ground. In this manner, the ball is sent behind the player, usually as a shot on goal, while the player falls to the ground on her back. This type of kick is obviously very difficult to execute successfully, and consequently not seen very often in youth soccer. When a bicycle kick is performed effectively, it typically represents a rather spectacular play. A bicycle kick is also at times referred to as a *rainbow* because of the movement of the kicking leg which forms a rainbow-like arc over the player's head. Somewhat similarly, a bicycle kick is sometimes referred to as a *scissors* kick because the motion of the legs—the kicking leg swinging past the other, out-stretched leg—resembles the movement of a pair of scissors when opened.

Club linesman

A club linesman is a volunteer, often a parent, who functions in essence as an unofficial referee. Club linesmen (or women) typically are used when there is not a sufficient number of official referees present to begin a soccer match. The volunteer linesman is assigned one touch line with the primary duty of determining who should be awarded a throw-in when the ball crosses the respective touch line. However, rules for various soccer associations vary, and sometimes club linesmen assume other duties typically performed by official linesmen such as informing the field referee if an off sides rule infraction occurs. The term *club* linesman has its basis in the fact that the soccer club for which one of the teams plays provides the volunteer, or substitute, referee.

Drop ball

A drop ball refers to a means of restarting a match after the match has been temporarily suspended by the referee due to reasons other than one team having committed a rule infraction (in which case the restart would involve a free kick) or the ball having gone off the field of play (in which case play would resume with a throw-in, corner kick or goal kick). For example, the referee may temporarily suspend play because of a serious injury and then resume play with a drop ball. A drop ball involves the referee *dropping* the ball between two designated, opposing players who typically are facing each other. The ball is in play as soon as it hits the ground. In this manner the referee can restart the match without giving an advantage to one of the teams, as would be the case with restarting the match with a free kick.

FIFA

An abbreviation for the Federation Internationale de Football Association, an international governing body for the game of soccer. The basis for essentially all rules regarding soccer originate with *FIFA*.

Hat trick

The act of a player scoring three goals during one soccer match.

Header (get a head on it)

A directive to a player that a ball is approaching, or is likely to approach, in the air and the player should play the ball with his *head*. From an offensive standpoint the directive typically means the player should attempt to pass the ball with his head to a teammate or shoot the ball on goal with his head. From a defensive standpoint the directive usually means the player should use his head to send the ball away from the goal that he is defending.

Leave it (leave; let it run; let it roll)

An information statement given to a player who appears to be about to take control of a ball that is rolling toward her to *leave* the ball alone and *let it roll* past her. The instruction is usually provided by a player who believes she is in a better position to receive and/or kick the ball than the player to whom the instruction is directed.

Match

In contrast to most American sports, when two soccer teams, or soccer *clubs* in true soccer circles, play each other the contest is referred to as a *match* in contrast to a *game*. That is why throughout this text soccer contests have been referred to as *matches*. It should also be noted though that as Americanization of soccer continues, the term *match* is likely to be gradually replaced by the more colloquial term of *game*.

Own goal

A reference to a goal that is scored by a team against itself—a team puts the ball into its *own goal* net. The most common type of own goal occurrence is when a defensive player attempts to kick or head the ball away from the front of her goal and misplays the ball such that it unintentionally bounces off her into the net.

Shoot out

A *shoot out* refers to a means of breaking a tie score existing at the end of a soccer match. In a shoot out, each team is initially awarded a maximum of five penalty kicks, each of which is taken by a different player. Usually only players who have participated in the match can take a penalty kick as part of a shoot out. Some soccer association rules also specify that only those players who are actually on the playing field at the end of regulation play can participate in the shoot out. Players from the two opposing teams alternate in taking the kicks, with each respective team or coach determining which players will take the kicks. The team scoring the most goals during the shoot out wins the match. If, after each team has taken five penalty kicks, both teams have scored an equal number of goals, the shoot out continues with different players taking the additional penalty kicks relative to players who have already taken the kicks. At that point the shoot out typically continues until one team has scored more goals, given that each team has taken an equal number of penalty kicks. For pure soccer enthusiasts, a shoot out is sometimes referred to as a *knock out*.

Tie Breakers

Tie breakers refer to rules by which it is determined which team is awarded a win when a respective match ends in a tie score. Relatedly, tie breakers are used to determine a winner in soccer tournaments or league play when two or more teams end up with identical records. Because tie breaker rules vary across different tournaments, leagues, conferences, etc., there is no single rule to describe what will happen in a tie situation. Presented below are some of the more common means used to determine winners in tournaments and league play when two or more teams have identical records. However, two points should be considered before reviewing the most common tie breakers. First, most soccer matches that end in a tie score simply result in a tied match without any tie breaker process being implemented. Second, because of the frequent variations in rules regarding tie breakers, it is helpful if spectators inquire of soccer officials prior to a tournament or league play what tie breakers will be in effect if indeed a tie situation results after regulation play.

Common Tie Breaker Rules When Two or More Soccer Teams Complete League or Tournament Competition With Identical Records

1. Head-to-head play—if a team beat another team during regulation play, the former team is awarded the overall championship
2. Number of goals scored—the team scoring the most goals during regulation play is awarded the championship
3. Number of goals allowed—the team allowing the least number goals by opposing teams during regulation play is awarded the championship
4. Playoff results—teams play each other an additional time, usually for a shortened match duration, to determine the winner
5. Sudden death—teams play each other and whoever scores first wins

---

The rules just summarized regarding tie breakers should only be considered as general guidelines in terms of understanding how tied situations are resolved. There are numerous other rules that can be used, as well as various combinations of the rules just summarized. Again, the best way to determine which tie breakers will be used in a given situation is to inquire about the rules from a soccer official prior to the start of play.

Trap (trap it)

A trap in soccer typically refers to a player stopping the ball on the ground with his foot, or *trapping* the ball between his foot and the ground. Hence, an instruction to *trap the ball* is intended to inform a player he should control the movement of the ball by first stopping it on the ground, and then advancing the ball in a controlled fashion by kicking, dribbling or shooting it. This instruction is often given when a coach or player believes another player(s) is not controlling the ball very well and simply kicking it on the roll whenever the player approaches the ball. It is considerably harder to control the movement of the ball when it is kicked on the roll relative to after a player has first trapped the ball. Another type of trap that is less frequently observed and more difficult to perform than controlling the ball with the feet is a *chest trap*. In a chest trap, the player essentially catches the ball with his chest and then brings the ball to his feet in order to advance or shoot the ball.

Section 3

Selected Readings

and

Index of Common Soccer
Terms and Phrases

Selected Readings:

Books About Soccer

Ager, D. (1995). **The Soccer Referee's Manual**. London, Eng.: A & C Black.

American Sport Education Program. (1991). **Coaching Youth Soccer**. Champaign, IL: Human Kinetics.

Bauer, G. (1990). **Soccer Techniques, Tactics & Teamwork**. New York: Sterling Publishing Company.

Brown, M. J. (1986). **Soccer Rules In Pictures**. New York: Perigee Publishing Group.

Davies, P. (1994). **Twenty-Two Foreigners In Funny Shorts: The Intelligent Fan's Guide To Soccer And World Cup 94**. New York: Random House.

Dreayer, B. (1994). **Teach Me Sports: Soccer**. Santa Monica, CA: General Publishing Group.

Fairbanks, J. A. (1983). **Illustrated Soccer Rules**. Chicago: Contemporary Books, Inc.

Federation Internationale de Football Association. (1994). **Official Rules of Soccer**. Chicago:Triumph Books.

Glanville, B. (1993). **The Story Of The World Cup**. London, Eng.: Faber and Faber, Ltd.

Goldman, K. (1995). **Soccer Rules: A Player's Guide**. London, Eng.: Blandford.

Grant, J. (1983). **The Ins & Outs Of Soccer: An Illustrated Guide For Coaches, Players, And Parents.** Englewood Cliffs, NJ: Prentice-Hall, Inc.

Hamilton, I. (Ed.). (1992). **The Faber Book Of Soccer**. London, Eng.: Faber and Faber, Ltd.

Herbst, D. (1994). **Sports Illustrated Soccer: The Complete Player**. Lantham, MD: Madison Books, Inc.

LaBlanc, M. L., & Henshaw, R. (1994). **The World Encyclopedia Of Soccer**. Detroit: Visible Ink Press.

Lauffer, B., & Davie, S. (1991). **Soccer Coach's Guide To Practices, Drills & Skill Training**. New York: Sterling Publishing Company.

Learmouth, J. (1979). **Soccer Fundamentals: Basic Techniques And Training For Beginning Players.** New York: St. Martin's Press.

Luxbacher, J. (1995). **Soccer Practice Games**. Champaign, IL: Human Kinetics.

Luxbacher, J. A. (1996). **Soccer Steps To Success**. Champaign, IL: Human Kinetics.

Luxbacher, J. A., & Klein, G. (1993). **The Soccer Goalkeeper: Fitness, Skills, Tactics, Drills**. Champaign, IL: Human Kinetics.

Marco, J. S., & Aschermann, K. (1987). **Coaching Kids To Play Soccer**. New York: Fireside.

McCarthy, J. P. Jr. (1990). **Parent's Guide To Coaching Soccer**. Cincinnati, OH: Betterway Books.

McGettigan, J. P. (1987). **Soccer Drills For Individual And Team Play**. Englewood Cliffs, NJ: Prentice Hall.

Merrill, C. (1993). **The Grass Of Another Country: A Journey Through The World Of Soccer**. New York: Henry Holt and Company.

Murray, S. (1994). **Go For The Goal! Techniques And Strategies For The Complete Soccer Player**. New York: Fireside.

Meredith, S. (Ed.). (1981). **Soccer Skills, Tricks & Tactics**. Tulsa, OK: Hayes Books.

Phillips, L. (1996). **Soccer Goalkeeping: The Last Line Of Defense . . . The First Line Of Attack**. Indianapolis, IN: Masters Press.

Reeves, J. A., & Simon, J. M. (1981). **The Coaches' Collection Of Soccer Drills**. Champaign, IL.: Leisure Press.

Rosenthal, G. (1984). **Soccer Skills And Drills**. New York: Charles Scribner's Sons, Macmillan Publishing Company.

Simon, J. M., & Reeves, J. A. (Eds.). (1994). **Soccer Restart Plays**. Champaign, IL: Human Kinetics.

Simon, J. M., & Reeves, J. A. (1982). **The Soccer Games Book**. Champaign, IL: Leisure Press.

Stewart, P. (1995). **Way To Play Soccer: The Full-Color Guide To Maximizing Your Skills**. Rocklin, CA: Prima Publishing.

U.S. Olympic Committee (1995). **A Basic Guide To Soccer**. Glendale, CA: Griffin Publishing.

Waiters, T. (1990). **Coaching Youth Soccer**. London, Eng.: A & C Black.

Index

right wing, 17
rip it, 72
running off the ball, 69
runs, 16
save, 82
scissors kick, 93
see what you have, 75
send it, 68, 71
serve it, 65
service, 65
settle, 71
settle it, 71
shadow, 83
shadow him (her), 83
she's off (he's off), 81
shield, 72
shoot out, 95
shot, 72
shot from the 18, 23
show, 72
show for it, 72
slide tackle, 84
space, 69
square, 72
step up, 83
stick, 84
stop, 83
stopper, 15
stopper back, 15
striker, 17
support, 72
sweeper, 15
sweeper back, 15
switch fields, 64
switch it, 64
tackle, 78, 81, 84
take him (her), 70

ABOUT THE AUTHOR

Denny Reid has been a soccer coach, referee, parent, and spectator for 15 years. He has coached two classic soccer teams as part of the United States Youth Soccer Association and over 20 youth recreational teams. His soccer teams have included boys and girls ranging from 4-year-olds just beginning to play soccer to 17-year-old, all-state high school players. He has likewise worked as a certified referee in classic and recreational soccer leagues. Denny is also the parent, and spectator, for two soccer-playing sons.

In addition to his involvement in the game of soccer, Denny Reid is an experienced author, having published over 75 articles and authored or co-authored four books. Denny currently directs The Carolina Behavior Analysis and Support Center, Ltd., and resides with his wife, Helen, and sons, Cason and Nate, in Morganton, North Carolina.